A SCOTSMAN'S WAR

POST OFFICE TELEGRAM

Charges to pay
s. d.
RECEIVED

8.40 m

From

NO.
OFFICE STAMP

MELROSE
12 DE 41
ROXBURGHSHIRE

Prefix. Time handed in. Office of Origin and Service Instructions. Words.

£4 7.20p Liverpool OHMS. 52 To

(6) 4(7)

Dr. J. G. Coutts.
St Aidans Manse.
Melrose Roxburghshire

Regret to inform you of report received
from Middle East that Second Lieut.
J. B. F. Coutts Royal Artillery was placed
on dangerously ill list on 21st
November 1941 suffering from multiple
shrapnel wounds face
Letter follows. Under Secretary of State
for War.

For free repetition of doubtful words telephone "TELEGRAMS ENQUIRY" or call, with this form B or C
at office of delivery. Other enquiries should be accompanied by this form and, if possible, the envelope.

How my parents heard about my 'multiple shrapnel wounds face'. Note the date of the telegram—I was wounded on 21 November, but the first they knew about it was 12 December! They wouldn't know at this stage if I was dead or alive, and were in a terrible state of suspense

A
SCOTSMAN'S
WAR

Ben Coutts

THE MERCAT PRESS
EDINBURGH

First published in 1995 by Mercat Press
James Thin, 53 South Bridge, Edinburgh EH1 1YS

ISBN 1873644 477

Typeset in Bembo 11 point at Mercat Press

Printed in Great Britain by
The Cromwell Press, Melksham

Dedication

I would like to dedicate these war memoirs to four of my travelling companions, from Port Suez to two hundred miles south of Ascension Island where the *Laconia* was sunk. They are Lady Grizel Wolfe-Murray, Doris Hawkins known as 'Freckles', Sally Readman who would be fifty-four this year had she survived the torpedoing and last, but far from least, my friend and saviour Bertie 'Jock' Miller. Sadly, none are alive today.

Contents

Illustrations

Acknowledgements

I don't know whether to thank or curse my brother, Brigadier Frank, but it was he who suggested, nay cajoled me into it, that I set down my wartime experiences which I had conveniently swept under the carpet for half a century. If the book sells well (and so far the returns on my writing efforts have barely covered my expenses, as people seem to borrow books either from friends or a library!) then I'll thank my wee brother. If on the other hand it doesn't and all I'm left with are the sleepless nights I've had recently re-living the night of chaos when the *Laconia* was sunk, the pain of the sun and salt water on my all too tender skin in the days that followed and the dread of the next operation during my hospital stays etc. etc., then curses will be in order!

Thanks, as always, to my wife Sal.

To my old pal and fellow Sergeant-Major Arthur Dubbs, whose memory of the early days of the war is much clearer than mine.

To Doctor F G Smith in Australia, whom I knew as Gunner Smith of the Surrey Yeomanry Battery, for sending us the excellent photos of the Eritrean Cavalry and the Quad, limber and 25-pounder gun.

To Mr Frederick Grossmith, author of the book *The Sinking of the Laconia*, and Paul Watkins, the publishers, for their help and for providing the photo of 'Freckles' Hawkins complete with her OBE, a most richly deserved honour. Thanks to the owner of the photograph, her sister Mrs Norah King, for allowing us to use it.

I used my hero Wilfred Thesiger's book on the Sudan and Abyssinia to help refresh the ageing sawdust that constitutes what should be my brain!

Molly Burton, nee Davidson, is going like a bomb and kindly lent me her mother's diary, and herself told me about her experiences in the Casablanca prisoner-of-war camp. She is the only survivor of the *Laconia* of my acquaintance with whom I am in contact.

Dear 'Freckles' Hawkins told me that if ever I was to write up my experiences I had her full permission to quote from her book *Atlantic Torpedo*, published 1943, price one shilling! and now long out of print.

My sister Maisie, as always, came to the rescue when it was found that the photo taken of me and my non-existent nose back in No.8 General Hospital, Alexandria, was too blurred to reprint, and made a sketch of it. The reason it was blurred was that I had detached it from my medical records to show to someone on board the *Laconia* and had slipped it into my great-coat pocket where it got all too much of the sea water that splashed over us from time to time.

Thanks to Jack Armstrong, the Medical Officer on the *Princess Beatrix* and still very much alive and kicking and retired in Yorkshire, whose memory of the North African Landing I had to rely heavily upon.

Once more Isabel Johnstone has done a magnificent job of typing my manuscripts, all impeccably produced and on time!

And finally and far from least my thanks to the team at Mercat Press, Tom and Seán, with whom I have struck up an extremely happy rapport. They are the professionals whereas I am still an amateur, but they now respect me enough to come down to the main desk at James Thin's instead of asking this old codger with my 'dicky ticker' to climb the endless 'coronary stairs' to their pigeon loft where they work.

To all the above my grateful thanks: I only hope the information, advice and help you have given me has been used to make a readable book.

One
THE SUSSEX YEOMANRY

I joined the Sussex Yeomanry not for reasons of patriotism, but so that I could get an annual holiday!

Back in the thirties times were hard, there was mass unemployment, and unlike today when students with good degrees are doing menial jobs, the one way to be sure of procuring a job in 1935 was to possess a degree. I had scuppered my chance of getting one by failing my first year veterinary exams brilliantly not just once but even after a resit!

My long-suffering parents had three others to educate, so I fled the nest and took a job as a groom in Sussex working for the Hon. Mrs MacDonald-Buchanan, owner of 'Black and White' whisky, whose father, Lord Woolavington, had bred two Derby winners, 'Captain Cuttle' and 'Coronach'.

It was a homesick and lonely laddie who got off the train at Petworth Station in Sussex to be met by the estate handyman. He left me in no doubts that those who were to be my fellow-employees were not amused that a minister's son from Scotland, with no stud farm experience, should have got the job. Did I realise that the work entailed seven days a week for the princely sum of two pounds per week and no holidays? That I would be expected at foaling time to 'sit up' with foaling mares at least once per week and probably twice, for two shillings and sixpence per night? That mares coming to visit the stallions would arrive at this station where he was picking me up, and we, the stud hands, would have to manhandle the heavy rail horse waggons (all beautifully leather-padded I might say) into the siding, unload the mares and walk them back to the stud, a distance of four miles, again for two and sixpence!

I passed that station this year, and realised what an architecturally fine wooden building had been 'Beechinged'—but the Station pub where we spent all too much of our hard-earned half-crowns was still there (as beer was only fourpence a pint, a half-crown went a long way!)

After I started to work on the stud I realised that Tony Farr, the bearer of all the bad news he could concoct, was a born moaner and shirker, but the one thing that did worry me was the fact that one couldn't get a holiday. This was borne out when I asked for a day off to sing with the Midhurst Choir at the Petersfield Festival, and although it wasn't a busy time of year my request was refused. I was a wee bit upset, as I had cycled from Graffham to practise at Midhurst at least once, if not twice a week, a distance of six miles! Even after nigh on sixty years I remember the madrigal we practised again and again, it was called 'Sir Eglinor Was a Gallant Knight...'

The choir won their section of the Festival, but I never forgave the Stud Groom, and I did something I have never done since, I went over his head and asked for an interview with the Estate Agent, Brigadier Turner, who got me the job in the first place. I say I have never done this since, as I am a great believer in chain of command. The army is a grand example of this, as are the estates I have managed, where one has the owner, the factor (agent in England), head stalker, keeper or farm manager and then the workers on the ground. It always annoyed me if someone with a grievance went over my head to moan to the boss on any of the estates or farms I managed, and I've managed ten since the end of the war. But I was always delighted to take any employee to the boss as long as I could be present to give my side to the 'moan'.

The 'Gineral', as Brigadier Turner was called by the men, because in pre-war days Brigadiers were given the full title of Brigadier-General, was completely out of touch with the workings of a stud, his men or their living conditions, in fact I have since wondered how he ever got the job. His giving me a job is an instance of how insensitive and out of touch he was. He had come back to Sussex from a grouse-shooting holiday with a wealthy friend and announced to the stud groom that he had engaged a Scots lad who had been head ponyman on the estate where he had been shooting. Little did he seem to realise that there were any amount of local lads who could have done with the job. But who am I to complain that the main use of his head was to keep his ears apart? That job taught me so much about hard work, getting on with others, care and treatment of stock, being able to feed oneself on not much money and, most importantly, discipline. Oh, I know the Stud Groom couldn't stand me and I secretly despised him, but I always jumped to his every command because he was the Boss, and that was that, although we stud hands knew that it was his second-in-command who really ran the stud.

So I was lucky to have a job, but I wanted a holiday. When I told the

The Petworth and District Rifle Club with the 'Loder Shield', won by them in 1938 in competition with 46 other teams. The author is second from the right in the back row, and Captain Shakerley-Ackers is on his right

General this he said, 'Well, Coutts, why don't you join the Territorials and then I'll have to let you off for a fortnight's camp?' It so happened that apart from singing in the Midhurst Choir I had shot with the Petworth miniature rifle club which had won the 'Loder Shield' for the top rifle club in Sussex. Our Captain was one Shakerly-Ackers who was in the Royal Sussex Regiment and knew the General. It seems that Captain Shakerly-Ackers had said he could do with me in the Royal Sussex Territorial Battalion, to which the General had rightly replied, 'You can't have a stud hand as an officer'. Although I had served in the Officer's Training Corps at school, and shot for them at Bisley two years running, the thought of getting into mess dress of regimental 'blues' in the bothy, the cat-calls and derision from my pals, and then setting off on a bicycle was more than I could stomach, so I said, 'Sorry, not on, Sir'. To which he replied, 'I'm sure my friend John Cowdray would take you into his Midhurst Troop of the Sussex Yeomanry'. And so started one of the best things that ever happened to me in my seventy-nine eventful and happy years.

The Yeomanry then was a lovely feudal set-up, with Lord Cowdray as the Troop Commander, his farm manager Jay Gingell as the Troop Sergeant Major, Wally Stringer, the estate handy-man, who was later to become a great friend and adviser to me, as the Troop Sergeant, and Arthur Dabbs, who was Lord Cowdray's chauffeur, as a bombardier. He finished up as a fellow Sergeant Major and is still with us, thank the Lord.

Since I live in Scotland it is quite a costly business to go to London, not only because of the fare, but because of the money one spends when one is there—it is so annoying to be someone who enjoys a champagne and oyster life-style on a beer income! But I do enjoy attending regimental reunions in Chichester when I can, and one of the reasons is that I love the county of Sussex. Looking back to those days I spent in the bothy in Lavington I realise what a difference there was between the austere upbringing most Scots families had compared with those in Sussex. The climate must have a lot to do with it, as there was no doubt that the Scots who went south, especially in farming, did extremely well. I was shocked how badly farmed some of the land was. I always remember an old farmer whom I occasionally met in the pub. He had a super farm, south-facing on the Downs and on chalk land, and I said to him, 'Your land is just made for growing barley' (as barley and lime are like gin and tonic, they just go together!)—he replied, 'My father farmed this place for fifty years hand-milking a few old Shorthorn cows and keeping a few Southdown sheep, and he had a happy life, so I'll do the same'. This man hunted twice a week, attended cricket matches at Arundel Castle, point-to-points, polo matches at Cowdray Park and kept the local pub, 'The White Horse' (pronounced locally as 'The White Arse'!) going with his pals. Need I say, shortly after the war he went bankrupt. But I couldn't get over how relaxed and easy-going the farmers were down there compared with Scotland.

Then there was the forelock-pulling that went on among many of the English working folk on the land. When we were out at pheasant shoots and I used to load for the General, many of the beaters wore smocks and all pulled their forelocks to the 'gentry'. What a difference to we independent bloody-minded Scots! I remember well when I was factoring the Glenkinglass Estate up Loch Etive for the late Lady Wyfold, and the resident stalker lifted his fore-and-aft bonnet and bowed as Lady Wyfold stepped off the boat. The head stalker standing beside me, a great character and ex-Scottish Horse veteran, said, 'Look at that bloody Arab!' Mainly we are a proud race, sadly sometimes to our detriment. The whole way of life down there was so much more easy-going than it was up here. The licensing laws were more relaxed—whereas up here it was 5 p.m. to 9 p.m. each evening and no drinking at all on Sunday, unless you could prove you had travelled five miles, whereupon you signed a book (and all too many 'Wee Free' elders' names I found in one book!) But, down in Sussex, Sunday was a social day.

Yes, life was much more easy-going down there and there was a lot more money, but what's new? The difference then was that we in Scotland and those in the north of England, unless in London-based firms, knew nothing of the affluence of the south, whereas today all too many teenagers are attracted to that town like moths to candles, only to land up on the streets or as drug junkies. For me, one night in London just to see old pals is enough, but I still remember the night in 1937 when Ken Gilkes, stud groom on the neighbouring Burton Stud owned by the Courtauld family, and my good self, went on motorbikes (each of which cost five pounds!) to his younger brother's twenty-first birthday party. It was held at the famous Lyon's Corner House opposite Charing Cross Station, and we went on to see the 'Crazy Gang' at the Victoria Theatre. Because we were to finish the night there we parked our bikes beside the station where they remained for five hours! Just imagine doing that today!

But back to the Yeomanry, and I well remember that first camp when Wally tried to instil into me the intricacies of a 'dial sight' by which the 'number three' of a gun team aligns the gun onto the given target. The reason I never passed my veterinary exams was that the first year subjects were all to do with maths, and to this day I can't add two and two! And here

I was back to something that had all to do with that subject! As to the great day when I became an officer and was in charge of a 'director' which was controlling the fire-power of àt least four guns, all I can say is thank God for the A.C.s, the assistants, who all too often had to keep the officers right.

I'll never forget my medical when I joined the Yeomanry, as it was carried out by a lovely man called Geoff Sparrow, who was well known in Sussex for his love of country pursuits. When I came into his surgery I was amazed to see him in breeches and hunting boots (and he had two Jack Russell terriers on the bed that was meant for patients). He looked at my papers and said, 'Are you the Coutts who played rugby for Horsham last week?' When I answered in the affirmative, he said, 'No use looking at you, we can do with your sort'. Little did he know I have the most ghastly flat feet! Yes, I got the odd day off to play rugby or football if it suited the Stud Groom, but for singing NO WAY.

Geoff Sparrow was the real old type of country doctor we could do with today. I was told by his locals in Sussex, whom I met after the war, that he would turn out at any time of the day or night no matter how atrocious the weather, and would follow up the case until whoever it was had fully recovered. But woe betide the malingerer who feigned illness to get off work, as he got short shrift! Changed days indeed, when I hear that in our local practice in Central Perthshire at Christmas our doctors were being called out for common colds etc. When it comes to the New Year the mind boggles as to what the calls will be for!

But Dr Sparrow would have had them sorted out. I remember well, being by then a Sergeant, lining up a lot of cockney lads who had been sent to us to fill our ranks, and what grand lads they were, to get their T.A.B. (typhoid) injections. Dear Geoff, dressed as always in riding breeches and hunting boots, was jagging them with needles (unsterilised, and sharpened, his orderly told me, on the wall!) while telling me what a marvellous hunt the Southdown had the day before as one after the other of those poor recruits passed out in front of him!

Just pre-war the Surrey and Sussex Yeomanry, sadly no longer with horses, were the 98th Field Regiment Royal Artillery, and had the old eighteen-pounder guns of the First World War. Although there were no horses, the Sussex Battery mainly consisted of men with mud on their boots, whereas the Surrey Battery had a large number of bank employees. Like me those chaps got a free holiday, and obviously as a result someone high in command in all the major banks was keen on the defence of this old country! Let's face it, in the thirties there was a huge wave of pacifism. My father, who served for two years in the trenches in the '14–18 War, had become a pacifist and was not amused when I joined the 'Terries'. His two great friends and Church of Scotland ministers, both with Military Crosses, namely George MacLeod and Archie Craig, the founders of the Iona Community, had become pacifists. So it was a brave man in the thirties who backed the Territorial Army or anything to do with our military forces. Thank God they did, as without them I wouldn't be writing this today, nor would you be reading it.

By the end of 1938 I realised that the great, and conceited, dream of me becoming a stud manager was a non-starter and that I had come to the end of the road on the Lavington Estate. Looking back after all these fifty-seven years I now know how lucky I was to have had the chance to stand on my own feet, to work hard and learn the hard way about feeding and tending stock. Not only were we looking after some of the best thoroughbred horses in the country, but in our so-called 'off-peak' periods we had to help out on the farm with their Sussex cattle and Southdown sheep, making hay which to this day I reckon is the best feed a ruminant animal can get if made the way we did it then. But we are no longer in the thirties, and in our day it was labour-intensive, which sadly seems to be a nasty word nowadays.

So in 1938 I decided to leave and take a job managing a small farm near West Grinstead. The job was set up for me by a very dear friend, Robin Fisher, who belonged to Balquhidder in Perthshire and had come south to manage an estate near Horsham. Like many managers of that pre-war era he led from the front, and because his farms were low-lying and on clay soil, his long days spent topping and tailing mangold wurzels and generally working in the rain went for his old legs, and in his last years his legs were not good. I wonder if you notice in market towns up and down the country how many old men are crippled, walking with sticks and obviously in pain. All too many are ex-farm workers who were made to work in atrocious weather with but poor clothing to protect them against our notorious inclement climate. I remember well in one of the jobs I had pre-war, when every wet day in harvest was used to turn the 'stooks' of sheaves so that they didn't sprout, and after the first five minutes turning the first few sheaves one was soaked through. But in retrospect I'd rather do that while chatting to A. N. Other in the next row of stooks than be sitting in an over-heated tractor with Radio X, Y or Z going full blast.

The job Robin had found me was to look after a wee farm that had been completely neglected, with hedges hopelessly overgrown and molehills the like of which I'd never seen before. As an old pal said, 'At least you'll get a larger grazing area than if the ground was flat!' I was soon to learn that the farm had been bought by my employer, who was certain there was to be a war, for his son so that he would not be called up to the colours.

The farm was clay land, and a field of wheat had been sown by the previous owner. I had learnt in my time in Sussex that clay land and wheat were made for each other. Pre-war very few areas of Scotland grew that crop, and where it was grown it was more for the straw, for thatching stacks or covering potato pits.

Nothing had gone right for me in this job. I couldn't get implements or contractors, feeding stuffs or the sort of stock I wanted; the farm van, which because my pay was not good was a perk, was always required by the son leaving me on my own miles from my pals. In fact the job was a disaster. However, as in the old time Western movies the cavalry came over the hill to save the situation. The boss, his son and I were loading wheat sheaves onto a bogey and Fergie tractor (borrowed, I might say, from a neighbour, thanks to me) when a postman came running over the field with a telegram for me which read 'Report Chichester forthwith for mobilisation'. I don't think I've had more pleasure in my life that sticking my old-fashioned two-pronged hayfork in the ground and saying, 'I'm off to the war'; whereupon my boss said, 'You can't do that, what about my farm?' I replied, 'You know what you can do with your farm, and your son'. So began the four years that were to mould the rest of my life.

Two
THE PHONEY WAR

Looking back now it's just amazing how unprepared the country was for war in all too many areas, and yet in others a lot of homework had been done. I suppose because of the large pacifist vote there was no way any government could improve the armament of the Regular Army, far less we 'Terries' (the Territorial Army). On the other hand they had organised the necessary machinery for warning the country of impending air raids and of ensuring the blackout, which everyone hated. This, along with queuing for food, were the two things I hated most about the civilian restrictions in this country during wartime. Having said that, I wish in this year 1995 some of those who are protesting about the export of live animals, without a clue of an animal's sensitivity to so-called pain because they've never worked with them, how I wish that those same protesters had to stand in a queue for a few hours for an ounce or two of food, and I'll bet they would change their tune very quickly!

We, the second line of the Surrey and Sussex Yeomanry, were made the 144th Field Regiment, but as the 98th, the first line, had gone off with the only guns and rifles we had, we had to start again from scratch. The guns we had were the old First World War eighteen-pounders and 4.5 howitzers and the few rifles were the trusty old .303 Lee Enfield. I was assigned to 'B' Troop in Horsham where we were billeted in an old wooden hut. What a lovely age that was, as one just expected to live rough and anything better than a damp palliasse of straw was sheer luxury. But having said that, and being one inclined to pontificate against the young and their disregard for law and order, I remember with shame in hindsight when two or three of us sergeants were told off by a policemen for singing 'Sussex by the Sea' at the tops of our voices after a pub crawl that we told 'the boy in blue' to get into khaki and get stuffed! At least our song was clean, but next morning when we were admonished by the Battery Commander we were a very abject lot of laddies (because that's all we were, with one helluva lot to learn about the big wide world).

Then on the first day that war was declared we, 'B' Troop, were in church when suddenly in the middle of the parson's sermon the air raid sirens went. I must have been the senior ranker as I know I had to shepherd the troop out of church. It must have been devastating for the preacher but was of great relief to his congregation as he was one of the sort, and there are all too many, who say 'and finally' and then go on for a further seven minutes. The air raid sirens, the Air Raid Warden Service, the Balloon Barrage against the bombers and the anti-aircraft batteries were all well organised pre-war, but on that famous occasion on the first Sunday of the war it was a false alarm.

After our short stay in Horsham it was off to Hove, where the 144th Regiment was to be brought together on the famous Hove County Cricket Ground. Apart from the hallowed 'square' of the area between the stumps, we used the rest of the pitch for square-bashing, i.e. foot drill, and with ancient civilian trucks and even more ancient guns we tried to simulate what we would do with quads, limbers, modern guns etc. The more I think of these days the more I marvel that we eventually won the war! There were no official billets so we were all boarded out with families in Hove who were absolutely marvellous to us. Although one's memory dims after all those years, I can't remember any serious complaint against the Battery's behaviour, and when we left after a winter at the cricket ground there were tears all round!

We in the Sussex Battery were always a bit jealous of the Surreys, whose Sergeants had a mess at the Rallie Hall whereas we had our meals above the pub—cooked, I remember all too well, by a Regular Army cook who could make the best ingredients taste appalling! So the usual meeting place was the 'Brunswick', a pub where 'Hetty' the landlady was kindness itself to us, and where we got all too much free beer by playing the 'Muffin Man' and landing some poor civilian to pay the round. To those who have not played this game, this is how it goes. The person who starts off the song, usually me, puts a full pint of beer on his head (we had practised for ages with pint pots full of water) and turns to one of his companions, who has also trained at keeping a pint on his head and sings: 'Do you know the Muffin Man, do you know his name, do you know the Muffin Man, who lives down Drury Lane?' The person to whom he has turned puts his pint on his head and replies: 'Yes, I know the Muffin Man, yes, I know his name, yes I know the Muffin Man who lives down Drury Lane.' If the replying person drops his pint he has to 'stand his hand', i.e. pay for the next round of drinks. We used to organize so that all the first half dozen people to whom we pointed were

The 25-pounder gun and crew. This gun, a howitzer, was one of Britain's war-time success stories, and revolutionised the part played by the Royal Artillery in World War II as compared with World War I

those who had practised the game. After this we pointed at some poor unfortunate civilian who invariably dropped his pints, amid shouts of 'pints all round!'—and this kept us in free beer.

Keeping the troops fit was hard work. We had forced marches, and thank goodness I was given a strong voice as 'MacNamara's Band', 'Sussex by the Sea' etc. kept us going. There were squash courts at the Cricket Ground, which was a game totally unfamiliar to most of us who had been on low incomes, but my goodness, we soon found out when we played it how fit you had to be. We also had super rugby and soccer teams: the former I was proud to vice-captain. The captain, Tom Mann, of the famous brewing and cricketing family, died in the Sudan. The stand-off, one Eddie Edmonds, was in the mould of Phil Bennett, but I never heard of him post-war. Norman Savours, our full back, got a Military Medal at Keren but I fear didn't come home. But what a morale-booster that side was in the year when we had no proper material with which to train, and yet one had to keep morale high, not an easy thing! T.E.W.T.s (Tactical Exercises Without Troops) are all very well in peace time, but try to keep young eager lads who have volunteered to fight Hitler and his Nazi domination busy with these and you're on a hiding to nothing.

One of the memories I hold dear of that winter was of a sonsie barmaid in a pub in Brighton. Don't worry, Sal, my daughters, or anybody else, there was no hanky-panky in fact (until our last night in Brighton when I gave her a farewell peck on the cheek) but she introduced me to the joys of—not what you're thinking, dear reader—pickled walnuts. As a Scot I'd never seen them before, far less tasted them, but how well they go with cheese, and to this day I thank her for it as I do love them.

It's quite extraordinary looking back that we had Hove and Brighton to ourselves. Of course there were residents whose houses were all blacked out at night, and as many were 'waiting for God' they didn't move after dark. Luckily for those of us in uniform there were some younger 'civvies' who were either waiting to be called up, were in reserved occupations or felt guilty that they weren't in uniform, and luckily for us, as I say, they unwittingly supplied us with beer, thanks to the 'Muffin Man'.

But it was during the day that one saw the real difference. Because of petrol rationing there was virtually no traffic, and I regularly used to march my troop up to the 'Devil's Dyke' pub, taking up the whole road and never passing or being passed by a vehicle. I went there in the nineties and was nose-to-tail with other cars, and to say the ambience of the pub has changed is to put it mildly.

We had constantly in the early days fed the 98th (Surrey and Sussex Yeomanry), our number one line stationed in Worthing, with good material. On the other hand, we of the 144th, the second line, little realised that because of the draft of Cockneys we got from Woolwich during that winter we were getting just about the best amalgam of troops any commanding officer could wish for.

But at last we were wanted and were posted to Dursley in Gloucestershire in April, having spent all of the first winter of the war in Hove and Brighton. That winter, weather-wise, as 'oldies' of my generation will remember, was a hard one and even the sea froze on the coast around us where fresh-water rivers met it. All good things come to an end, so after our spell at Hove County Cricket Ground, with drivers being taught on clapped-out contractors' lorries (gosh, I bet the contractors made a bomb), gun teams being trained on antiquated guns and most of the Battery H.Q. staff not having a clue about Army regulations, we were off.

I remember well that the Battery Captain had been ordered that, in the event of our being sent overseas in a hurry, he was to tell the members of the Battery, in case of their death, that they ought to have things sorted out before leaving. In my troop I had a super driver called Weiland, who was the scruffiest man on parade in the whole troop. His side-hat was always at a quarter to three instead of half past twelve, which as I'm sure you know means ear to ear instead of nose to nape! He had a straggly semi-ginger moustache and he never seemed to be properly shaved. I, as Sergeant Major, had to bring them in before the interrogating officer with the usual, 'Hat off, left turn, quick march, halt, Gunner Weiland, Sir'. I will never forget what followed. Battery Captain: 'I suppose you realise we are about to go overseas and the possibility may be that you won't come home, would you consider asking the Army to donate anything that was due to you to your next of kin?' To which Weiland replied, 'Sir, I've left my mother ten thousand pounds in my will so I think she'll be all right'. (Ten thousand pounds in 1939 is a million today!) But I knew Weiland wanted to be nothing else but a quad driver and he was super at that job.

So at last we got our move to Dursley in Gloucestershire which would be our happiest base as a regiment for a number of reasons. Firstly, we were properly equipped with the 'tools for the job'. The twenty-five pounder was acknowledged world-wide as the best field gun in World War II, and we were privileged to be one of the first units to be issued with them. To quote my fellow Sergeant Major and good friend, Arthur Dabbs, 'It was the hardest ten days I've ever put in in my life, as we had to be on the firing ranges at Okehampton before 9 a.m., do our firing, get back to camp, clean the guns we had used, draw new guns, degrease and sight test them ready for the next day's firing, and it was often midnight before we got our orders for the next day's firing.' Thank goodness you were the Sergeant Major put in charge of that lot, Arthur, as I was never the gunner that you were. Then at Dursley we had two regular Battery Commanders posted to us, Major E.C. 'Bob' Mansergh to command the Surrey Battery and Major A.G. 'George' Munn the Sussex. And what an upset that caused, you would have thought the end of the world had come. 'Regular soldiers to a yeomanry regiment, it's unheard of' was the shout, but it was the best thing that ever happened to us. And then the people in Dursley were so nice to us. Their own yeomanry, the Gloucestershire Yeomanry, were already overseas, and they kindly took us to their hearts, but their local 'scrumpy' cider didn't take as kindly to the Sussex Yeomen's tummies and all too many got flattened by the potent brew! Our lads were used to Sussex beer, and pretty wishy-washy stuff it was, with not much alcoholic content, whereas the 'scrumpy' had a kick like a mule.

It was in April that we had moved from our 'winter quarters' in Hove and Brighton down to Gloucestershire, and what a lovely time of year it was to see that lovely shire. Sadly when I return, which I do as often as I can, no longer can I have the selfish pleasure of having the roads to myself. As a Sergeant Major one had a motorbike and one had to reconnoitre gun positions, camp sites, recreational possibilities like local cricket, football or dart teams that wanted to play us etc., etc. (and occasionally the odd nice wee country pub that might be of use for a lunchtime stop while on exercise!) Oh, I remember better than many things of fifty years ago the sheer bliss of that spring: the peewits, the sky larks, the bird-life that was in abundance then before the area turned to cropping, the smell of grass as the sun started to dry it off, the munching sound that cows make when they are getting stuck into that first spring flush of grass, and later the loveliest of all smells, that of new mown hay. Perhaps it was made all the more special because we had been told we were to be sent to France, where there was a massive withdrawal afoot, and this could be my last chance to hear the sounds and smell the smells I loved. The sad thing is that now, because we all want a higher standard of living, farming has changed, the roads are blocked in the country by drivers who think they are at Brands Hatch, and my grand and great grandchildren (yes, I have some of them too) will never have the pleasure that I and many of my generation derived from the countryside.

But back to war time, and as I said we were lucky not to be sent to

France. Being in a relatively safe area we received quite a lot of units evacuated from Dunkirk. The difference in those we received was quite staggering. Some, as can happen in any country and in any unit, were hell-bent on getting home—a very natural thing for anyone is to save 'number one', oneself. But I was in charge of collecting the last lot we befriended from the railway station. They were a cavalry unit, grey with fatigue, and arrived three weeks after the first lot we took in, but every one had his firearms. I'll never forget the lecture we got from our Regular Majors the very next day on how essential discipline was in the British Army and that this was a prime example. I must say the lesson went home to our unit as nothing else had done before.

Sadly we said goodbye to our good friends in Dursley on 24th June as we, one of the few regiments that was fully equipped, were needed to defend the south coast. We were sent to Hambledon House in Hampshire. From what I've learnt later I think our regiment, which was in 'dug in' gun emplacements, was covering Portsmouth and goodness knows what else. Thank God Hitler never knew how scarce our resources were or how sparse our troops.

We had another move that July to Broughton. Our Second-in-Command, not our favourite officer, had an estate close to our gun positions, and as it was harvest time he asked me if I would organise a 'gang' of Sussex Yeomen to sort out his harvest. Well, we didn't think much of him as an officer, but you should have seen the mess his estate was in! Of course from our point of view it was great getting back to the things that we really knew about. The Major's ancient retainer stood transfixed as the squad I'd picked got to grips with that harvest, and getting to grips wasn't easy as there were all too many thistles in his crop. The old retainer, one of a marvellous race of whom we see all too few today, was of course bred on the land and fondly recalled how things had been done 'in the old days' when the old Colonel was alive! How often I was to hear similar expressions from 'old retainers' on the Scottish estates I was to manage post-war. Well, this old boy reckoned he hadn't seen better stacks in their corn-yard for twenty years or more.

Seems strange to someone of my age that so few people today know what corn stacks look like, but no wonder when you think that in 1945, after I had been invalided out of the Army the year before, I was managing a farm whose owner was trying out one of the first combines which was pulled by a tractor and that's fifty years ago this harvest! But then labour was cheaper than it is today—and happier. A good stacker was an artist, and of course the stacks made sense in farming terms, as one was cutting the crop with a binder, then stooking it and stacking it so that by the time it was ready for threshing it had had the sun and the wind, and I know I saw better examples of grain in those far-off days than I do now. Lest, reader, you think I'm digressing from the war, I am not. Feeding the nation became very critical at that time, and the great cry was 'Dig for Victory'. The U-boats were strangling our supply of cheap food which, as we then still had colonies that could produce cheap food, we imported from overseas.

From Hambledon and Broughton where we had been independent and guarding huge areas of the coastline, we were moved to Amersham on 22nd August where we became part of the Fourth Corps. It seemed strange after nearly a year's training on our own to became part of an organised Corps. As the Surrey and Sussex Yeomanry we had lived a lovely secluded life of our own, and I remember the undercurrent of resentment at becoming part of the great British Army. We went on our first exercise as part of the Fourth Corps, and looking back I shudder to think how many 'balls-ups' we made. I know I had been sent off on my motorbike to reconnoitre a route for the guns and got hopelessly lost. This was all too easy to do as there were no signposts, which had all been taken down in case of an enemy invasion, and just try reading a map when you're riding a motorbike! Worse still, when I actually led the guns to the appointed rendezvous I got lost again. So all-in-all that famous exercise of the Fourth Corps was not one of Sergeant-Major Coutts' greatest moments!

Another thing I remember about it was a certain senior officer called Bernard Montgomery, who made himself immensely unpopular by making officers, many of them pre-war volunteers and not in the first flush of youth, do violent exercising and run vast distances. I'm sure he was right in that half of our Army was not physically fit for war, but it was the autocratic, tactless way he went about it that put many hackles up!

Post-war I was to get to know a certain Betsy MacDonald who was Monty's wife's best friend. It seems Monty literally harried and besieged the lass who was to become his wife. They all met up skiing, and of course like everything else he did Monty skied well. Monty had to have his own way and eventually his wife-to-be gave in, but as Betsy MacDonald said, 'they were ill matched'. One was either a pro-Monty or an anti, there was no grey area. As I never fought under him and disliked the way he curried favour with his troops I was an anti: although many whose opinions and fighting ability I admire were pro. My pin-ups were Dick O'Conner, Archie Wavell, the Auck, and of course 'Brookie' Alanbrooke. What would have happened to the outcome of the war without Brookie's great common sense and his ability to steady some of 'Winnie's' dafter ideas should make us all appreciate how lucky we were to have a senior Army officer in that position. He longed to be 'in the action', like any Regular soldier would, but was resigned to a job that was to collect nothing but brick-bats for himself yet was to do such a fantastic amount towards winning the war. A great man, who to my mind never got the acclaim he should have done. But then Monty was before his time, as he was the start of the 'bullshitting' type so beloved by our present media whereas Brookie just did his job brilliantly, but quietly.

Whether we were unsuitable for Fourth Corps, although compared with the other gunners we came across we were much better trained and officered, or whether there was an S.O.S. from the Middle East for a trained gunner regiment to take the place of a regiment of the Fifth Indian Division, as a mere Sergeant Major I wouldn't know—but I do know that after a year of the phoney war we were ready, willing and able and rarin' to go to war.

Three
GOING OVERSEAS AT LAST

The news that the 144th Field Regiment, Royal Artillery (Surrey and Sussex Yeomanry), were at last to be sent overseas after a frustrating year was greeted with jubilation by all ranks. What is it about a certain type of Britisher that makes them feel they must be 'in the action'? It was particularly evident in the 1914-18 War when men queued up in droves to go to the front to be slaughtered, for that's what it was, and were terrified in case the war finished before they got there. In a minor degree it happened in the 1939-45 War: as, for example, in my case I turned down the opportunity of being commissioned when I heard the regiment was being posted overseas, and yet when I got home there was any amount of farmers who boasted to me that they were in a reserved occupation and had to stay at home to feed the country. I wouldn't know who was right, but suffice to say that Sergeant Major Coutts and all his merry men of 'Beer Troop Sussex Yeomanry' (well named I might say), were straining at the leash. As we were issued with khaki cotton shirts, shorts, and topees (sun helmets) we reckoned we were going east, but there is nothing certain when it comes to the Army High Command. My brother Frank's Division, the 52nd, were trained in Mountain Warfare in the Cairngorms and were sent into action on the flattest bit of Holland!

We were to embark at Liverpool, and were very upset when we heard that the ship on which we should have embarked had been bombed. But how lucky we were, as it turned out, as the skipper and crew of the *Highland Brigade* on which we eventually sailed were kindness itself, and apart from a company of sappers we had the ship to ourselves. While awaiting embarkation orders we were stationed on the famous Aintree Racecourse. There we whiled away the time playing 'pontoon', and that's the only time I've ever made money at Aintree as I never seem to do any good backing the Grand National!

The *Highland Brigade* had just docked with a load of chilled Argentinian beef, and so had to be 'defrosted' before we went on board, but for days after we sailed the troops near the hull reckoned they were the chilled beef! We were lucky that we weren't part of a convoy, which meant we were able to travel at a fair rate of knots, and we heard later that the convoy with which we should have sailed lost two ships. I had never been to sea before, if one excepted going 'doon the Water', the Clyde, for a summer cruise to the Isle of Arran. I took to it like the proverbial duck, and when we had a really rough crossing of the Bay of Biscay only two out of forty-five were in the Sergeants' Mess and yours truly was one. Some were really ill, including our gallant Battery Commander, Major Munn, who but two months earlier had told us we 'must die with our boots on'. He ignominiously 'fed the fishes' in front of the whole Battery—which I, as the only Sergeant Major who was still on his feet, had been ordered to get on parade in no matter what condition—and all I can say is, thank God we didn't have to go into action that day.

Our first stop was Freetown on the West African coast, and what heaven that sun on our backs was after a dreary British winter. The local 'bum boats' swarmed round selling the usual rubbish, and there is no one more gullible than the British Tommy. The thing we were all suckers for was the divers who shouted for coins that we threw into the sea and then dived to retrieve them—they were brilliant. Oh, I know a half century (and more) adds to the nice things one recalls, but I will always remember the sight of those lithe young bodies diving what seemed to me a terrific depth, against a sand background and with the sunshine slanting through the greenish but clear water of Freetown harbour. This to me was to be the beginning of a short involvement in the Middle East campaign, but it was also the start of a love of travel and of seeing other countries, their cultures, cuisine, habits, climate etc., etc. that has never left me.

Our next landfall was Cape Town, and it would be impossible for anyone not of my generation to realise the thrill it was to arrive in that harbour with all its lights blazing: remember we had left a blacked-out Great Britain, where even a chink of light qualified for a night in the clink!

It was not only the lights, but that magnificent backcloth of Table Mountain with its famous tablecloth of mist; a sight that I will cherish all my life, and little did I realise then that I was to get to know and love that country as I do. It was lucky for our regiment that we were the first to be allowed ashore from our convoy, as there was a huge convoy of cars waiting to take us and show us Cape Town, plus feeding and watering us with food and drink the likes of which most of us had never tasted before. To this day I

The view of Cape Town from across the Bay: the famous Table Mountain in the background with its equally famous Tablecloth about to descend on it. When we saw it first it was all lit up and looked magical to us who had just left the British black-out

love the Cape red wines (perhaps too much). Sadly, in the previous convoy that had disembarked were some Australian convicts, released, we were told, on condition that they went to war (probably they were descendants of the British convicts sent to Australia to colonise that country!) Go to war they did, with a vengeance, when they stopped off at Cape Town en route for Suez, running amok after all too much beer. It was because of the shambles they caused that the officials in Cape Town asked our convoy to put ashore a regiment that knew how to behave, and we were more than 'chuffed' to be chosen. Our officers disappeared like 'snow off a dyke' (a stone wall) as we say in Scotland, leaving the Sergeant Majors, as so often, to sort things out. I wonder, fifty-four years on, what became of those two lovely blondes who cosseted Quartermaster Sergeant Jock Murray and Battery Sergeant Major Coutts? Talking of Sergeant Majors taking control, I had great pleasure in singing to my youngest daughter, when she was commissioned in the Royal Transport Corps, a ditty that I had to sing to the officers when they were invited for their annual visit to the Sergeants' Mess:

Now the officers look at their little red book
(or they don't as the case may be, Sir)
But it's not to them that the Major looks
(When he finds he's up a tree, Sir)
When he's turned the Battery inside out,
I'm willing to lay a wager
That he'll go to the head of the ranks
And shout, 'CARRY ON SERGEANT MAJOR!'

These lovely blondes were not only delightful but had brains, and realising both Jock and I were fond of and knew about the land, took us out into the country to show us something of the farming. I was staggered at what could be grown when one has the right climate, the right soil and the expertise, all of which South Africa has. As I scribble these remembrances of those far off days (a) I remember well feeling that the sword of Damocles was hanging over the white farmers and their Apartheid policy and (b) how in old age I'd love their climate as a gale with sleet engulfs this cottage while I write. What an eye-opener that glimpse of South Africa was to the whole regiment, who from Colonel to latest-joined recruit talked about it for months. This was because although the South Africans had two divisions in the field fighting for the Allies, Cape Town was living the life of Riley! Whereas we, who were also part of the allied force, were having our homes bombed. We had many Cockneys in our regiment and they were worried stiff about their parents in London, who at best were on meagre rations and who all had to put up with the awful soul-destroying blackout. I remember getting a letter from mother saying 'Betty brought us a dozen eggs, wasn't that kind?' I knew the inference was that Betty would make me a good wife (if I got home) as long as she kept the Manse supplied with eggs!

Then it was up to Port Suez where we disembarked, and the regiment parted from their guns and vehicles which had to be painted in camouflage colours suitable to the desert and not green as we had in dear old rural England. Almaza Camp, which was to become huge before the end of the Desert Campaign, was only in its infancy then and we were stationed there until we got our marching orders. We were told we were 'Army Troops' i.e. we could be attached to any Division who were in need of a Regiment of Artillery. It so happened the Fifth Indian Division had to leave India minus one of their gunner regiments because of an outbreak of some disease or other. The 'Fifth' were in the Sudan/Eritrean battle against the Italians.

Looking back on those days aboard ship I realise now even more than I did then how difficult it was to keep the troops employed. There were endless lectures, mostly boring, but some from our more senior members who had seen action or had held down an interesting job in civvy street. I always remember with gratitude Major George Munn lecturing us on the possibility of being torpedoed, and what we should have in our haversack should it happen. His advice was to save my life two years later. I remember too the lecture given by a Medical Officer about the brothels in Cairo, when he said, 'Some of you would put your willies where I wouldn't put my stick'!

Strange how sex rears its ugly head in every walk of life. Judging by T.V. programmes nowadays it's the number one interest in the land. Makes me think of the silly story of the Army psychiatrist who was interviewing lads for a job: he had some powder in his hand and gently blew it into the air, following the cloud it engendered with his eyes. He then said to his first applicant, 'What does that make you think of?' To which the reply came, 'That lovely old steam-engine that passed by morning and night'. 'Well done lad,' said the examiner, and repeated the same thing to applicant two, whose reply was, 'The steam that came out of Mother's old kettle which always sat on the hob'. This answer also got a favourable reply. Then he moved onto the third applicant, and when he asked him, as the powder drifted upwards, 'and what does that make you think of?' the reply was, 'Sex'. To which the examiner said, 'What makes you think it has anything to do with sex?' Back came the reply: 'I never think of anything else'.

Cairo, as the regiment was to learn, catered for all tastes—whether one wanted good food, drink, sport or sex, you name it. Egypt was divided between those who loathed the British, like the Egyptian government and their army, and those who were in business. As trade was booming these gave us welcoming smiles no matter what their real feelings were. After all the British troops were about to employ thousands of civilian workers. History has shown what the Egyptians' real feelings were, with their anti-British uprising in 1952 organised by Nasser and backed by many of his fellow army officers. As a postman's son he didn't do too badly, except that he authorised a motorway along the bank of the River Nile which I'm glad I've never seen. When we arrived in 1940 the walk along the Fouad El Awal Street to cross the Bulac Bridge to Samalek on Gezira Island was like something out of another world that one had read about but never thought one would see. Donkey carts, camels, beggars, a few, very few big American Buicks honking their horns, just the whole world wandered down to the river that must be the most famous of all rivers. To stand on the bridge and watch the dhows and faluceas (the small native boats) with their sails flapping as the evening breezes dropped and against a setting sun was a sight I shall never forget.

Cairo, then, was a city that for most of our regiment had everything. After all we had left a country that was blacked out, severely rationed for food, and all too many towns were being bombed. But in Cairo the officers were made honorary members of the Gezira Club with its lovely facilities, swimming, polo, tennis, and their race meetings where, as my officer Bob Maxwell, a horse trainer, described it, they raced 'little white mice' (white Arab stallions).

Then there was the famous Shepherd's Hotel where the 'John and Tom Collins', that famous Middle East gin cocktail, was second to none, and if one wanted to see belly dancers, where better than Madame Badia's Cabaret? Fly-whisks and desert boots were the order of the day for all officers, as were bush jackets tailored in a matter of hours by first-class tailors. The desert boots have remained popular after all these years, and I'm sad to say that I no longer wear heavy leather brogues as I would like to do to back the hide industry, but these same desert boots—or 'Brothel Creepers' as they were called by the rankers—as they are so much lighter on old feet.

As for the rankers in Cairo, it was a paradise with the Egyptian pound virtually on a par with the pound sterling. For five shillings an officer could get a six-course dinner at Shepheard's, but a ranker could get a three course meal with beer for one shilling! Something he had never had at home as cheap and never would have again! Yes, that short period in Cairo was for many 'the life of Riley', and for all too many the last time they would enjoy the good life.

One of the extraordinary things about the British Tommy is his magpie nature, and the 'souks' or outdoor markets of Cairo had all sorts of things never seen in Britain. These were bought up eagerly by the lads, some of whom wouldn't be home for five years and some sadly who would not see home again. When the going got tough a lot of the stuff bought during that heady first visit to Cairo was jettisoned. Looking back, one can't blame the lads for buying what was really a load of old rubbish, as everyone had heard of the markets of the Middle East, with all their mystique, and the craftmanship that was still there, and there was money burning in their pockets. It was a case of 'Wot the 'ell, let's spend it, send it rolling along' to quote the old song 'We're in the money'. The only other thing they had spent their money on had been playing 'Housey, Housey' on board ship. To younger readers this game is now called 'Bingo'. Our sessions were run by our Quartermaster Sergeant, the chap who is in charge of the stores and all equipment. In the old days a Quartermaster Sergeant was reckoned not to have done too well out of his job if he hadn't made enough to build a row of flats when he quit the service!

Looking over our shoulders at the flesh-pots of Cairo we set off for Khartoum in the Sudan. The troops went by boat down the Nile to Wadi Halfa and then by ancient train to Khartoum, while the guns, trucks etc. went down the Red Sea to Port Suez. I suppose if you have lived on the land you not only love it but you judge the land you see in other countries against your own. I had thought the land around Cape Town terrific, but my goodness when you see the famous Nile Delta with that wonderful soil washed down by that famous river for thousands of years, you realise why this comparatively small area of land has fed a vast number of people for a vast period of time. How I'd love to do that river journey again, but I doubt it's not to be, as 'anno domini' has caught up on me and the anti-tourist unrest in Egypt is frightening.

My lasting memory of the train journey from Port Suez to Khartoum was of my batman, one Blott, an ex-bargee on the Thames, dashing up the line at every stop with a kettle in his hand to get the engine driver to fill it with boiling water—which in those old steam trains you could do—so I and my pals had constant tea. The other memory was of the natives at every stop, and they were countless, offering eggs (about the size of pigeons') for sale, which Blott bought for virtually nothing by the dozen, so we were never hungry. Then it was a case of Khartoum here we come.

Four
THE SUDAN

Philippa, my daughter, who got her degree at Cambridge University and had a good job in a public relations firm in London, came to me one day and said, 'Dad, I'm off to the Sudan with "Christian Outreach" working with Eritrean refugees'. I can't say I was surprised, as she is very like my old and wise father who was full of good works, dead honest, with no interest in money and completely impractical. But I was surprised that it was the Sudan, because when she came to me to break the news Rwanda, Somalia and Ethiopia were much in the news with regard to the refugee problem. Next it was, 'Get out your atlas, Dad, so that I can see where I'm going', and like a dutiful father I did. My old atlas is vintage pre-war, when the Sudan was called the Anglo-Egyptian Sudan. Then there were places called British Somaliland, North and South Rhodesia, the Union of South Africa, Tanganyika, Nigeria, the Gold Coast and Kenya (then pronounced Keenya), all coloured red signalling that they were under British control: that was half the area of Africa, and from a productive point of view by far the best half! 'Where are you going to be stationed?' I asked her. 'Somewhere called Kassala,' she replied and then as I looked into the distance instead of at the atlas she said, 'Well, look it up'. 'There is no need to', I replied. That was the place where the 144th (Surrey and Sussex Yeomanry) R.A. entered the war.

What a small world—when one thinks of all the battle fronts in World War II, how extraordinary it is that, a half century on, my daughter should start doing her bit for this old country from the same wee Sudanese town that I started doing my bit, for what it was worth. It's sad to think that people knowledgeable on Sudanese matters say we, the British, should either have held on to control of the Sudan, or alternatively not have done so much for the Muslim controlled north, and so much less for the Christian south, as the pundits reckon this has escalated the friction that has caused the horrific war between north and south.

From Khartoum it was to Kassala that the regiment went, where the two batteries were split, the 390 (Surrey Yeomanry) joining Colonel Frank Messervy's 'Gazelle Force' designed to chase the Italians up the road into Eritrea. The Sussex Battery, 389, were sent to Gedaref with the 10th Indian Brigade under Brigadier 'Bill' Slim who was to cover himself with glory before the end of the war.

For those not conversant with the make up of the Army during World War II, a brigade was made up of three battalions of infantry, and in the case of the Indian Brigades they comprised two Indian Battalions and one British. The British Battalion that we came across was from the Essex Regiment, and one of the Indian Battalions was the 3/18 Garwhali Rifles and what magnificent fighters they were.

It always annoys me when people denigrate that campaign, as not only was it the first victory we had in the Second World War but I often wander if the critics realise that the Italians had one hundred thousand troops, and to begin with the British had but two thousand five hundred, with four thousand five hundred of the Sudan Defence Force officered by British officers—but what officers! For example, the legendary Colonel Sandford who at the age of fifty-eight did a forced march from Galabat, in the rainy season, that men half his age would not have attempted. Then there was Arnold Weinholt, Australian-born but educated at Eton, who had served as a trooper in the South African War and then won a D.S.O., plus an M.C. and bar. But after a spell sitting in the Australian Parliament, when Mussolini invaded Abyssinia, Weinholt's itchy feet got the better of him and he went to that country with the Red Cross. So he was prime material for the S.D.F. (the Sudan Defence Force), and he joined the 101 mission under Sandford, but sadly he was ambushed and killed. Also a legend for a different reason was Ron Laurie, who had won the Diamond Sculls at Henley the year before the war broke out and then went back to win them the year after the cessation of hostilities, a feat that can never be surpassed. He was officially District Commissioner at Gedaref, but during the war D.C.s did their stint in the S.D.F., which was lucky for me as his second in command, Billy McDowall, who had to remain in Gedaref, had been at school with me. He was more than kind to me, inviting me to dinner, supplying me with 'the water of life' which we Scots drink, be it in the Arctic or the heat of Sudan, and, perhaps best of all, providing a bath—what luxury in that dusty, hot climate.

Also in this élite company was Arthur Hanks, who with a very small detachment of the S.D.F. was to guard the frontier at Galabat until such time as Mussolini declared war on the Allies, which actually happened on 10 June 1941.

Posted to Hanks was Wilfred Thesiger who was always to be a hero of mine. What a man he is, some of his explorations are beyond belief. Born in Abyssinia and being a personal friend of the Emperor Haile Selassie he was an ideal person to be sent into the border area to infiltrate into Abyssinia, but it was before that he served under Hanks at the Fort of Galabat. He tells in his excellent book *The Life of My Choice* how when he heard on the radio that the Italians were in the war he and his platoon celebrated by firing their machine guns into Italian positions. Some hours later a directive came from Khartoum saying on no account (repeat no) were any of the allied forces to take offensive action against the Italians! Well done, Wilfred—once again you scored a first, not this time of exploring somewhere in the Middle East where no other European foot had trodden, but of being the first to fire shots in the Abyssinian Campaign.

As a Sergeant Major I was on detachment with the S.D.F. only for a short period to train some of them in Mountain Gunnery, and I would gladly have been seconded to them if asked. Yes, the Sudan Defence Force were a unit to be reckoned with, and one of the main reasons was the calibre of their officers. That's where the Italians suffered, as although they had Eritrean Battalions who were equally good fighters, their officers weren't a patch on those who commanded the S.D.F. No-one likes his creature comforts more than the author, but there's a time and a place. At that time in the war Thesiger was eating *wat* which is a highly seasoned meat sauce covered by *injera* which was made from flour of the seeds of *teff*, all local and served day after day! Whereas the Italian officers demanded that their cooks go with them, served wine with their meals etc. and wore silk pyjamas at night. I nicked a pair from an Italian prisoner of war, and cosy they were, but 'better for love than war' as the French said about the kilt in the first War!

Then of course there came to Galabat one Orde Wingate, whom most who will read this book will remember as making a great name for himself in Burma. One either admired or loathed the man. Although I only met him once, I thought he went a very strange way about the mission he was in charge of, i.e. to get the Emperor Haile Selassie back into Abyssinia. He took camels instead of mules and then loaded the camels too heavily, all against local advice; overworked the Emperor's Horse so severely that H.M. said to Wingate, 'I hope when we meet my subjects will know which of us is Emperor'; he never washed, had an untended beard and, as Thesiger writes, 'was not a figure calculated to impress the Abyssinian patriots who expect their leaders to look the part'; and, worst of all, although not keen on washing, he used to cool his bottom in the few water-holes that they passed on the way from Galabat to Balayia. His men had to drink from those same water holes after he had 'dunked' his backside in them! I can't think how anyone could serve under that man, but they did. Even Thesiger, who knew the country inside out and was a born leader, and was really backing Colonel Boustead to do the same job as Wingate did without causing the antagonism and disorganization that Wingate caused, says of him: 'He was the one with the originality of thought, boldness and single mindedness which was ruthless and there was no one else in Platt's force (coming from the north) or Cunningham's (attacking from Kenya) who could have achieved what Wingate did!' High praise indeed.

These then were but a few of the officers that we had in the Galabat area, and to my way of thinking were the reason why the British forces had such a terrific advantage over the Italians, who after all were holding all the high ground—not mere Scottish 'Munros' of three thousand feet, but mountains of six thousand feet and more, and solid rock all the way up to the summit.

But back to the action at Galabat. This was an old fort surrounded by 'hangars', semi-circular redoubts which Border shepherds would call 'stells' (for sheltering sheep in coarse weather). In this case they were extensions to the fort's defences, as until we came with our modern twenty-five pounders all attack and defence in that area had been by spears or ancient Remington rifles. Metenuna was a similar fort over the border, and was held by the Italians. This fort we hammered with our guns, and although as Sergeant-Major my job was back in the waggon lines I will cherish the remembrance of the day when our Battery Commander, Major Munn, decided to visit the observation post overlooking Metenuna and took me with him. He had been told that the communications between the observation post and the gun positions were not up to 'the standard to which he had become accustomed'. I was with him so that he had someone in authority who could carry out whatever orders he gave to sort out the problem. Within minutes we heard what was wrong. The signaller responsible for relaying the orders to fire the guns had the most useless voice. The Major said, 'Man that phone, Sergeant-Major'. As I was doing so, I suddenly realised that I had been given a gift—and it is a gift—of communication. After an hour's relaying orders which were bombing Metenuna into rubble, George Munn (as I was to call him post-war) said, 'For two peas Sergeant-Major I'd have you demoted and put you in charge of signals to train them how to use communications'. Very conceit-making, but he must have known something that I didn't, as I have at the time of writing been broadcasting, on farming matters mainly, but also on other subjects, for forty-seven years!

Other memories come to mind about our spell at Gedaref/Galabat. There was the sight of the Indian troops going down hand in hand to bathe in the Atbara. What would I, as a son of the manse, an ex-shepherd, farm worker and groom, used to nature with rams tupping ewes, bulls serving cows and stallions covering mares, know about homosexuality? I remember too the Sudanese showing us how to make our own *tukuls*, those little round huts made from long grasses and reeds which were so cool in the Sudanese sun, and which daughter Philippa was to make and live in fifty years later. Then I recall the envy of the Essex Regiment because we Territorials had got a twelve-bore gun or two with us (I had an ancient hammer damascus barrel Holland and Holland which would be worth a fortune today); and with these we were able to supplement the boring army rations by shooting bush turkeys and sand grouse. The latter were super when cooked on a spit. Most of all I remember that this was the time when the Battery became a unit and we realised what a good amalgam we were. The officers were from business and landowning backgrounds, the N.C.O.s mainly from banking or from the land, and the other ranks were that glorious mix of cockneys drafted in with our Sussex Yeomen—who were pure gold, but not the fastest or quickest thinkers in the world.

With Metenuna Fort flattened and the force there in retreat (always with the threat of the Abyssinians turning on them and attacking them from behind) plus the fact that the main and best part of the Italian army was advancing from the Eritrean capital, Asmara, down their excellent road to Kassala, we the 389 (Sussex Battery) were withdrawn to rejoin the 390 (Surrey Battery) and once more became the 144th Field Regiment.

While we had been on detachment at Galabat the Surrey Battery had earned a place in the history books, as they had actually been charged by a squadron, fifty strong, of cavalry, led by two Italian officers riding white horses. This must surely be the last cavalry charge on a British unit. The background to what happened was that the Battery was being deployed among thick shrub where they were to support some of the Gazelle force, mainly 'Skinner's Horse' (no longer horsed but with light tanks) and a unit of the S.D.F. The scrub was so thick that Kenneth Simmonds, who was Gun Position Officer of the 'D' Troop, had had to climb a tree to get a better view, but scurried back to his guns when he saw some of Skinner's Horse racing back through his gun position. Over at 'F' Troop, where George O'Farrell was in charge, troops broke through his guns saying, 'Re-

The Eritrean Squadron which took part in the last cavalry charge of modern times, all mounted on their gray horses—a frightening sight for those who unexpectedly had to face them

treat, retreat, the enemy are close behind us'. Full marks to Kenneth and George, no way did they retreat but took on the cavalry over open sights. This was something for which we hadn't been trained when we were issued with those lovely twenty-five pounders—we had never even been instructed how to engage tanks! The range was so short that the safety devices in the fuses operated by centrifugal force didn't have time to open, so all too many did not explode. The two Italian officers were both killed, as were twenty-three others, and sixteen were wounded, whereas the Surrey Battery casualty list was one person, who, after months in hospital, made a full recovery. Had the Surrey Battery not been where it was, even though the guns had just been unlimbered, that cavalry charge could have caused mayhem among the open-topped trucks of Skinner's Horse and the S.D.F. infantry who were coming up behind.

The officer in charge of the squadron, Captain Santasilia, was given a posthumous Gold Medal, the Italian equivalent of our Victoria Cross. Sadly, none of the Surrey Battery were put up for 'gongs'. Our Colonel, Henry Clements, was very retiring and never pushed the regiment as he could have done. I met him post-war when I was judging the Aberdeen-Angus classes at the Dublin Show at Ballsbridge, as he then lived in Ireland. He was my ring steward, but I was the one who had to sort out the tickets and rosettes, order the drinks and lunch, etc.—no wonder he couldn't organise a gong or two. According to those who were present on this historic occasion, no-one performed better than Jimmie McKinnie, who was the 'Tiffy', or Artificer, always a regular R.A. man, sent to keep our guns in order. Jimmie grabbed the one Boyes Anti-Tank Rifle, in which few of us had any faith, and wreaked havoc among the cavalry including knocking out the Captain. George O'Farrell (along with Kenneth Simmonds, still with us) was heard to remark that this was 'probably the only effective performance by the Boyes Anti-Tank rifle in the whole war'!

There was a nice sequel to this famous event when Baron Amadeo Guillet, who was in command of the regiment the 1st Gruppo Squadroni, part of which had carried out this famous charge, was guest of honour at the Annual Dinner of the Surrey Yeomanry in 1976.

So after their initial baptisms of fire as separate batteries the regiment as a whole were ready and able to play their very substantial part in the first victory for the Allies in World War II, i.e. the Eritrean/Abyssinian Campaign.

Five
ERITREA AND ABYSSINIA

It always amazes me how we Brits can denigrate success. This campaign was never acknowledged to be the victory it was because some forces later met Italian troops who were conscripted from the sun-loving south, and were dismissed as 'Wops'. We in the Fourth and Fifth Indian Divisions were up against regular troops, men of the Bersaglieri and Alpini and the Savoy Grenadiers, who were hardened soldiers. They were born and bred in the hills, so don't tell me they didn't know how to fight, as through the ages hill men have always had to fight to survive. Not only that, the Italian army had been in possession of Eritrea for many years and knew exactly where to defend that country, and as the hills rise up to six thousand feet they had every advantage that an army could wish for. And they were brilliant engineers. This was all too obvious when you left British-controlled Sudan, with its ghastly, dusty, sandy roads and went into Eritrea with its lovely tarmacked roads and superb bridges. Because they were such good engineers they knew where to blow up bridges and roads in order to cause our advance the most problems.

The reason this good fighting force never invaded the Sudan was simply because their officers liked the good life, and were rightly terrified that the Eritreans and Abyssinians would literally knife them in the back. And no wonder the native inhabitants of those two countries felt so sore about the Italian invasion, as back in October 1935, General Graziani, then commanding their forces in Italian Somaliland, had sanctioned the use of poison gas as he felt he was losing out to the Abyssinians. There is a telegram from Mussolini to Graziani on record which states: 'Authorised to use gas as a last resort in order to defeat enemy resistance and in case of counter attack'. Mustard gas was dropped on Abyssinian troops, who were superb fighters and could have contributed to this campaign much more than they did if they had been properly led and armed. But the Italians knew only too well that not only had they to face the British force from the north under General Platt, but also one coming up from the south, from Kenya, led by General Cunningham; not only that, but Abyssinian irregulars also would be snapping at their heels like hyenas trying to get in at a kill by a lion. So it was this sort of force that the Fifth Indian Division faced: well trained, holding the high ground, vastly superior in numbers and air support, knowing the country like the back of their hands, but I suspect in retrospect badly-led and looking over their shoulders in case the irregulars struck. However that may be, we, the 144th (Surrey and Sussex Yeomanry) went into war as a regiment, as 'Army Troops' taking the place of a regular R.A. regiment in the Fifth Indian Division, and although both batteries had been under fire this was the first time we were to operate together in action as a regiment.

The 'Gazelle' force to which the Surrey Battery had been attached under Colonel Frank Messervy had so harried the enemy that they started to withdraw up the road to two places that were made for defence, namely Agordat and Keren. Gazelle Force, with the 4th Indian Division behind them, captured Agordat and nearly forced a way through the very narrow Dongolass Gorge, but the Italians managed to blow it just in time and block it with a huge amount of rock, an easy task in this mountainous country for some of the world's finest engineers. However six thousand prisoners were taken, along with eighty guns, fifty tanks and four hundred trucks, not bad considering the real battle, that of Keren, was still to be joined.

In hindsight it is interesting to note that General Wavell, who was named by Rommel as 'the only British General who showed a touch of genius' and was dearly beloved, trusted and respected by his troops, gave so much significance to the battle of Keren that when he became an Earl his second title was the Viscountcy of Keren and his son, Archie John, was known as Lord Keren. And yet I find all too few Brits who have ever heard of it, and most haven't a clue where Eritrea is on a map!

That Keren was to be a formidable battle was obvious to all, down to the lowest ranker, as the town stood at four thousand feet above sea level and was surrounded by higher mountains, with Mount Sanchil on one side and Brig's Peak (called so because there was a cluster of crags set out like the crown and stars of a brigadier's shoulder badge) on the other. It was a bloody battle against, as General Platt who commanded the force said, 'the enemy and terrain'. The Fourth Indian Division started the offensive on 3 February. The Fifth Indian Division of which we were part were brought in on 15 March fighting an the other side of the road and storming Fort Dologoral. We, the gunners, never had it as tough as the infantry, and as a Scot I was more than proud that the Second Battalion Cameron Highlanders covered themselves with glory, but at horrific cost. In his excellent account of the battle Peter Cochrane, an officer in that battalion, tells the story so well, but he doesn't mention how he won a Distinguished Service Order for his part in the action. Suffice to say that he finished up with only half a dozen men remaining of his beloved 'C' Company, which must have started at fifty plus.

At no time in war should fighting soldiers be expected to supply their own troops, but it happened on this occasion. We required the four essentials. Water is the Number One. I remember in the valley where we gunners were it was hot enough, but up on the tops on sheer rock in daytime it was sizzling (though at night it would be freezing) and the ration was one pint of water per day, one lost more sweat than that! Number Two is the age-old food of the British Army, bully beef and biscuit, and how fed up we all got with it—though months later on a raft in the Atlantic I would have given anything for it! Most important of all they brought the ingredients of 'Char', Number Three. This is the name the Indian Divisions gave to tea, and it was literally a lifesaver as any medical officer will tell you. Char meant tea (strong), sugar (lots of it) and condensed milk. Number Four, of course, was ammunition. All these had to be portered up by one of the four fighting companies of the Camerons, who took turns to do it, but what a waste of a first-class fighting force. Their discipline in action was exemplary, and if an officer or senior non-commissioned officer was knocked out, the senior ranker, without any orders, took his place. The British Army pre-war, and that includes of course those super Indian Army soldiers, was second to none when it came to discipline, and there is no way Keren would have been captured by other than those disciplined men.

In Cochrane's wonderful description of the battle of Keren he is, I think, a wee bit hard on the gunners (luckily not us who were supporting the Fifth Indian Division on the other side of the road). He reckoned that all too often the infantry were shot up the backside by their own gunners. All I can say is that if one is laying guns to fire onto the crest of a hill such as those at Keren, the difference between dropping the shot on the enemy on top of a ridge, or just in front (i.e. on one's own troops) or just behind the ridge, is a very fine one, and sadly the odd shell does fall short. It depends on so many things, like did the lassie in the munitions factory put exactly the same amount of explosive into each shell? Or had she had a *contretemps* with the boyfriend the night before? Was the fuse properly set by someone with a hangover (hard to find at Keren), or not? Was the Forward Observation Officer certain of

That marvellous vehicle the 'Quad' four wheel drive. Not only was it home to the complete gun team of six and their equipment but it towed the limber full of ammunition plus the 25-pounder gun. The No.1, i.e. sergeant in charge of the team, was able, as shown, to pop his head through the roof to give orders to the driver

his distance? Did the Gun Position Officer get the correct orders, and most important of all did the Gun Layer lay the gun as he said he had when he reported to his No.1 in the gun team that the gun was properly laid and ready to fire?

In most accounts of the war infantry units are named as the heroes, and no-one is prouder than I am as a Scot to have been in a unit which supported the Camerons (for a short time) in Eritrea, the Highland Light Infantry at Massawa and the Black Watch in the Tobruk Garrison. In this role we were always just the Gunners and not the Surrey and Sussex Yeomanry of which we were I think justly proud. Suffice to say that at the battle of Keren nineteen Gunners' Forward Observation Officers were either killed or wounded, so they also did their bit.

There is, however, a ridge of those ghastly rock-strewn mountains, and they really are mountains, in Eritrea now named Cameron Ridge and justly so. That wonderful fighting force lost eight officers and two hundred and fifty other ranks in what most infantry Generals would think impossible— storming an impregnable position held, not by ice-cream wallahs, but by seasoned troops. As the remains of that battalion came through our waggon lines in all too few trucks, and with their pipers playing, not their regimental tune 'The March of the Cameron Men' but the lament 'The Flowers of the Forest', stronger men than Ben Coutts were openly weeping. The Italians launched no fewer than eight determined counter-attacks, but after fifty-three days Keren fell.

The Italians had used thirty-nine battalions and thirty-six batteries of artillery, which totalled thirty thousand men and one hundred and forty-four guns. They suffered three thousand troops killed and as many or more wounded, whereas our losses were five hundred and thirty-six killed and three thousand, two hundred and twenty-nine wounded, and among the dead was a good friend of mine. So the road to Asmara was open, and the conquest of Eritrea begun, but at a cost that was far from trifling, as those Fourth and Fifth Indian Divisions were terrific soldiers, hard as steel and trained to perfection.

We, the 144th, were to be the only Territorial Regiment in that highly successful campaign. Because of this, or perhaps because General Platt's aide-de-camp was a Sussex Yeoman who was to become a great friend of mine post-war, one David Reid, we were picked out to be reviewed by the General in Asmara, the Eritrean capital.

But before that there was another job to be completed. You can imagine the fantastic problems of supplying two Divisions with food, fuel, ammunition etc. when your supply route was some five hundred miles long and over some tortuous roads, so it was imperative that the Eritrean port of Masawa should be captured and held. The fear was that the Italians would have scuppered all their ships in it to make it unusable. Wavell desperately needed troops back in the desert, and soon he would need them for the abortive Greek campaign, one of Churchill's worst decisions of the war. So immediately after Keren was won the Fourth Indian Division was withdrawn but the Fifth pushed on to take Asmara and its much needed hospital, as there was a fearful outbreak of jaundice which very few escaped.

I knew I had the jaundice when we got to Masawa, where our battery were sent post-haste to support a brigade who were to take the port. Included in the brigade was a battalion of the Highland Light Infantry, and one of their officers, Desmond Henry, had gone to school with my younger brother. We met when I was up with an officer reconnoitring an observation post, and Des said, 'Come over tonight, Ben, and we'll have a dram and a jaw about old times'. When I was violently sick—after two drams!—I knew something was far wrong, and sure enough next day my eyes were yellow and the jaundice had started! No wonder jaundice and dysentery were rife. As anyone knows the worst thing for jaundice is a fatty diet, and when not on hard tack of bully beef (corned beef to the modern generation) hard tack biscuit, tea, sugar and condensed milk, one was on bacon in tins, and in the heat it was swimming in fat, as was the beef. I remember an Indian doctor telling me when I eventually landed up in Asmara Hospital that the only good thing we were getting in our diet was the tinned marmalade from Israel.

As for dysentery, on the Keren battlefield there were hundreds of bodies, not only of humans but also of mules which in the heat exploded and then were covered in millions of flies. The flies' next stop was one's mess tin when one was trying to eat, while at the same time swatting a swarm of hungry flies, so how could we avoid dysentery? Luckily as a regiment we didn't have to clean up a battlefield, but the poor Camerons after their magnificent part in the capture of Keren had to do just that. The story is told of an officer going round the 'Jocks' who were performing this most hated of all wartime tasks and saying to one of his men, 'How's it going, MacPherson?' and back came the reply, 'Aye, daein' fine, sir, but I've got twa buckshee heids!' Gruesome isn't the word for it, because in that barren land of Eritrea there was no soil for burial, just these huge rocks.

Masawa fell easily the next day and luckily the Italians hadn't scuppered too many ships in it, it was nothing like Tobruk that I was to see some months later where one literally walked ashore over sunken vessels. I would think the High Command must have been relieved to have Masawa in their hands, as had it remained with the Italians and been used as a submarine base I shudder to think what effect that would have had on the war in the Middle and Far East.

So it was back to Asmara for the battery and for Sergeant-Major Coutts a sojourn in hospital with jaundice. That fantastic bit of engineering of the road and railway from Asmara to Masawa was brought into focus for me when daughter Philippa made the journey a half century later. She was enthralled with the beauty of the scenery, the bird life and the amazing engineering skills of the Italians who had built the road and railtrack away back in the thirties. 'Didn't you love it,' she asked, little realising that all I was thinking about at the time was whether that dim-witted driver 'X' would fail to navigate one of the hairpin bends and land his 'quad', his limber (full of ammo), his twenty-five pounder gun and, most important of all, his gun team of six men in the ravine hundreds of feet below.

The old quad must have been one of the best things the war produced, mechanically—it not only had four-wheel drive in high and low ratio, it had a hawser for pulling one out of sand, mud, soil, you name it. It was also the home for the gun crew, and carried not only them but also their sparse belongings. I don't know, being completely unmechanical, how much the ammunition limber and the gun weighed, but it pulled them too. It was some work-horse, and we gunners loved it, but in the Middle East was it hot inside? One fried like an egg!

Before we left Asmara to harry the enemy down into Abyssinia we were, as mentioned earlier, to be paraded in front of General Platt. It was a Sergeant-Majors' parade i.e. we, instead of the officers, were in charge. Pre-war the Sussex Yeomanry had yellow and blue side caps, and George Munn, himself a Sussex man, was proud of his battery and made sure as many as possible wore their Sussex Yeomanry yellow and blue. I had just come out of hospital still showing signs of jaundice in my eyes, and the General said to me, 'It's the first time I've inspected a unit with yellow eyes and side hats to match'.

It was during that time in Asmara that Jock Murray and I, who had both turned down the chance of being commissioned before we left England because we loved the regiment, were told by the Colonel that we were shirking our responsibilities (we had both been members of our Officers' Training Corps at our respective schools) and that we were to go to Cairo for a crash officers' course for sergeant-majors and quartermaster sergeants.

*The author ploughing with African oxen. He managed one very wavy
furrow, but found that the oxen didn't seem to understand the Scottish
expressions used to guide horses at home!*

He told me in my interview that he had put my name forward with the proviso that he wanted me back, a fact of which I'm immensely proud. I did go back as an officer to the Surrey Battery, for all too short a time; not many rankers in the last war were commissioned into the regiment in which they served in the ranks.

The regiment went on down to Amba Alagi where the Duke of Aosta made the final stand, but after Keren where the fighting had been really fierce the resistance was never the same again.

So when the Fifth Indian Division attacked Amba Alagi from the north on 13 May, and with General Cunningham's South Africans threatening from the south and Wingate's Gideon Force having routed twelve thousand Italians from Gojjam and set Haile Selassie, the Emperor of Abyssinia, back on his throne in Addis Ababa, the Duke of Aosta, although in a strong defensive position with water, food and ammunition for three months, had no choice but to surrender. As Viscount Wavell's biographer says, 'Has any campaign in history lasting but two months produced from two divisions a fighting army commander, two fighting corps commanders, and seven fighting divisional commanders within four years?'

I and many others were proud to be in that little-publicised campaign which ended the Italian East Africa Colonial Empire. A million square miles had been retaken and Emperor Haile Selassie had been restored to his throne. The East African Campaign was Britain's first complete victory in the Second World War, and this country had to wait a long, long time before it recorded another.

Six
CAIRO AND TOBRUK

So it was back down the Nile for Jock and me. I've been back to Cairo once since the war and it has greatly changed: more cars, fewer donkeys and camels, the Egyptians more cocky than ever after their rising in 1952. I can see why they hated the Brits, but before and during the war a huge amount of their economy depended on this country. There was something fascinating to me about Cairo, the Nile, the souks (markets), the mingling of so many nationalities, the pleasant smells of spices and cooking borne on the warm evening air (but not the ghastly day time smells of which there were plenty). I suppose it summed up for me what I'd always imagined the Orient should be like, and to this day I want my memory of Cairo to stay that way, so I'm not going back; and judging by the way many tourists are being treated a lot of others won't be going back either!

I remember all too little about that officers' crash course as far as the instruction went, except that we seemed to be endlessly getting in and out of trucks and being transported miles and bumpy miles into the desert in stifling dusty heat. Our living conditions I do remember, as we were stationed in the ancient Kasr-el-Nil Barracks which had been in Cairo since time immemorial, biblical times I would think. It was famous for two things: first, its stone floors, which were so polished after centuries of steel-heeled army boots that one had a job keeping one's feet, and the story was circulated that more soldiers got knocked out by slipping on its floors than were knocked out by the enemy! and secondly, for its ferocious bed bugs. Those horrible little flesh-eating creatures used to wait until one was just asleep and then attack, not just in ones or twos, but dozens! We were sleeping on old army metal beds, and we used to set the legs in used tobacco tins filled with paraffin, but nothing daunted the wily wee bug(ger)s, which used to get onto the ceiling and drop from there! Poor Jock, who must have been a lot sweeter than me, had a terrible time with them, and many's the time I was wakened in the middle of the night with Jock doing a 'Bed Bug War Dance' on his bed, and his parents wouldn't have liked to have heard his language!

Another thing I remember about that course was being shown how to make out a cheque, as we were all made to open bank accounts. Seems strange now, when almost everyone has credit cards etc., but before then none of us had any spare cash to bank. Now, however, our wages were paid to us weekly in pounds, shillings and pence, so when not in the flesh-pots of Cairo or Alexandria or later in other big cities, the majority of troops had the first chance to save money. Thus officers were expected to open bank accounts and and hence had to know how to fill in and sign a cheque!

Among our sergeant-majors were two from the New Zealand Division, and what a cracking division that was. They decided while their men were being rested in the Delta to organise a rugger match between their division and a British team. Having played for Melrose in 1935-36 I was picked for the British team, and what an honour it was, as more than half the Kiwis were pre-war All Blacks, one of whom, Jim Wynyard, was to become a friend of mine until he was killed in his tank a year later, but of Jim more anon.

In Cairo then was the famous Groppi's. The French influence in Egypt was very strong, and their patisserie, to a Scot brought up on dear mother's shocking cooking (bannocks and hard scones), was just out of this world, and Groppi's was the tops. All too much of our money was spent there, or in the case of the one or two who had income from elsewhere it was spent on John or Tom Collins Gin Slings at Shepherd's Hotel. Those who drank these delightful cocktails found out later that their 'gyppy tummy' (otherwise known as the squits) was caused by the ice in their cocktails being made from Nile water!

Up until now I had had a 'cushy' war, and compared with many others in different spheres I was to have one up until the cessation of hostilities, when I think of those in Colditz or Changi, those who worked for the Japs on the infamous railway, or even the ordinary soldiers who were switched from one battle to another even after they had been wounded. But after my short sojourn in Cairo the enemy tried to kill me four times! And I had twenty-five operations, some of which were bloody sore, and after fifty years it's the first time I've admitted it, as my publishers (sounds fearfully grand) said they wanted my experiences 'warts and all'.

After the completion of the course those of us who were gunners (now officers) had to report to the Commandant at Almaza, and what a huge base it had become since we had first arrived the year before. Just imagine my joy to find Major 'Bob' Mansergh, lately Battery Commander of the Surrey Battery, now a Lieutenant-Colonel and in charge of the base, and even more joy when he said, 'You're booked to go back to 144 who are now in the Tobruk Garrison, and you'll be sent on the next detachment that goes.' 'Bob', as Lieutenant General Sir E.C. Mansergh, was to go big places before the end of the war, including being Commander in Charge of a large force in the far east, and after the war to become the 'Master Gunner', the highest honour that a member of the Royal Artillery can have bestowed on him. He gave me the great honour post-war of asking me to make the speech at one of the famous gunner dinners at Woolwich.

So it was off to join the regiment, who were part of the famous 'Tobruk Rats', defenders of the garrison against all comers, whom the Germans never managed to dislodge, and who were a constant thorn in the Africa Korps' flesh and did so much for morale in the Middle East. As Tobruk was being continually strafed from ground and air, all reinforcements of rations, ammunition and personnel were shipped in by night. There's a lovely story told about a certain absolutely fearless skipper called the Potato Skipper, who did this dreaded run with his boat full of rations, including potatoes, and was dearly loved by all, including the ladies of easy virtue in Alexandria. Sadly their establishment was bombed with terrible loss of life, including the skipper. His death notice duly appeared in the *Egyptian Gazette* and read: 'Died on active service, Captain XYZ'. I'm sure his family would like to know he had done his stuff, and certainly as far as the defenders of Tobruk were concerned, they worshipped him, as he was not afraid of anything.

The 144th had meantime handed over their transport and twenty-five pounders outside Alexandria at a place called Burg el Arab, which I was to get to know well later on. The regiment were naturally mystified, and the truck drivers and gun crews in particular were not amused to say the least. Just as stocksmen become fond of the animals they tend, even though they may be destined to be slaughtered, so the rankers who had maintained, yea even cosseted, their vehicles or guns became attached to them. However all was to be revealed on 18 September when the regiment was embarked on two Australian destroyers, the *Nizam* and the *Napier*, en route in the dark for Tobruk. There they took over sixty pounders in support of the Ninth Australian 'Divie', as the Aussies called their divisions. This was a super fighting force, completely different from the division that took over and tried gently to wreck Cape Town at the beginning of the war. That Ninth 'Divie' and all who served alongside them in 1941 felt sore when next the Afrika Corps attacked the Garrison after the Aussies had been relieved in November, 1941, and a South African division gave in, they felt, rather tamely.

Getting reinforcements into, and tired troops out of, Tobruk was a brilliant combined operation between the Navy, the Royal Air Force and those in the Garrison. There were two dreaded menaces to the defenders: a huge siege gun called 'Bardia Bill' and the Stuka dive-bombers, the screeching noise of which as they dived I can still hear when I have a troubled night's sleep. The Navy with a cruiser and two destroyers would set out from Alexandria and arrive outside Tobruk just before dark, up to which time the R.A.F. fighters would give them cover. When the ships were an hour from Tobruk bombers took off from Egypt knowing that the Axis airmen wouldn't operate if there was no moon and wouldn't dare light flares while R.A.F. planes were overhead. Meantime a bombardment of 'Bardia Bill' by sixty and twenty-five pounder guns was ordered, and one of the escorting destroyers would also add its gunfire to silence the great 'Bill' (although to the best of my knowledge he was never completely silenced!) The R.A.F. bombers would then drop parachute flares, and the destroyers and cruiser would glide in and unload alongside the sunken craft that formed the 'wharves'. Within only half an hour a thousand men and one hundred to two hundred tons of stores could be unloaded, and one thousand men taken on board, and then they would steal away into the night. What a feat of organisation, what efficiency and what bravery. What's happened to all those talents we used then, now that we can't even get the Q.E.2 ready on time for a winter cruise costing millions of pounds?

The destroyer that took me to Tobruk was the *Kipling*, sister ship to Earl Mountbatten's famous *Kelly*, and captained by Captain St Clair Ford who had played rugger for Scotland pre-war. His Medical Officer had gone to Glasgow High School, and when I went on board he recognised me and took me up on the bridge, which was great, because as you can imagine a fighting vessel is not built to accommodate an extra few hundred passengers! The skipper it was who told me how intricate was the planning required to keep Tobruk supplied.

It was great to be back with the regiment, and although I had spent most of my time with the Sussex Battery I had had a short spell back in Britain with the Surreys as a Troop Sergeant-Major because they were short-staffed for a bit. I always remember an incident during that short period, when the Surrey Yeomen Sergeant's Mess ran a dance in their headquarters, the Ralli Hall, beside Hove Railway Station. A hall was something we, the Sussex Battery, didn't have, and we always felt a bit sore about it! We had a regimental clerk who was a bit short-sighted but was, it seems, rather attractive to the opposite sex. At the dance in question he was sitting with an officer's wife with whom he had just danced, when an officer came into view. As he was short-sighted dear old Sergeant Reid said, in all too loud a voice, when the officer was almost upon them, 'God, it's that ghastly Captain X, let's dance!' Back came the reply, 'Yes, let's, it's my husband and he can't dance.'

But back to Tobruk where the defence of the garrison had been immense! One can stand a lot of bombing, shelling and strafing, but lack of drinking water is one of the worst things that can happen to anyone, as I was to find out later. Strange how we in this country take it for granted and yet don't preserve it as we ought. I was talking to the stalker in Glen Etive, Argyll, who keeps a measure of the rain-fall, and he tells me that 1994-95 is a record at an incredible one hundred and sixty inches. My response was to bet if we got a dry summer people would be bellowing for water to sprinkle on their lawns or wash their cars, the latter a complete waste of time to my way of thinking! As I thought, it has happened in this summer of 1995, when all too many are moaning about the water boards and not doing a darned thing to conserve their own supply. In Tobruk water was a scarce commodity at half a gallon per man per day, and that was for drinking straight, as tea, for all ablutions and for washing clothes etc. One got used to it, but when someone came up from Alexandria with a bottle of real water and a bottle of whisky the recipients drank the water neat and left the whisky! (perish the thought!) However the Germans suffered the same problem, and as one officer wrote in his diary, 'the water looks like coffee and tastes like sulphur'.

As for luxuries, it seems incredible in the nineties that the number one choice was cigarettes! The Australian Comfort Fund who did such a magnificent job in supplying comforts to all troops in the Garrison, not only to their 'ain folk' but to the British and Indians as well, were rightly upset that cigarettes were the number one priority on their canteen ships, as not only did the troops get fifty free per week, but they usually bought at least another fifty from the canteen. Some must have bought many more, as the average per man who went to the canteen was three hundred and twenty per week, an amazing figure in this day and age, but what else had we to do except repulse the enemy, something which happened in fits and starts. At least the Aussies were able to put to rest the legend that the diggers couldn't do a proper job unless they got their beer, as the ration was roughly half a pint per man about once a month! As one Aussie said, that's 'not enough to lay the dust'. Another, the son of 'Banjo' Paterson who wrote 'The Man fron Snowy River', summed up his views on the beer shortage with the following:

There's militant teetotallers,
Who abhor all kinds of drink,
There's wives who break good bottles,
And pour them down the sink,
This place would suit them to the ground,
We've searched in every nook,
But booze is rare as hens' teeth, in
This place they call TOBRUK.

It was strange, to say the least, to go back a step as it were, that is to get used to commanding a troop of gunners manning sixty pounder guns having been one of the first regiments to have been issued with twenty-five pounders. In fact on our arrival in the Middle East we had to instruct some regular units in the use of twenty-five pounders, much to their disgust, as until they saw us in action the regulars had no time for those they called 'Saturday Soldiers', i.e. the Terries. Two of the snags of the sixty pounder were that its rate of fire was slower than the twenty-five pounder, and secondly, instead of a gun team of six on the twenty-five pounder one needed eight on the sixty pounder.

At least the bread we got was fresh, since there was a bakery in the Garrison, and as Francis Smith of the Surrey Battery wrote in his book *One Gunner's War*, 'the bread had added protein in it in the form of weevils'. We also had Aussie butter, which was a tremendous improvement on our ghastly British margarine, which was 'only fit to put in my grease gun' as one of my drivers said to me.

Tobruk Garrison was not 'a cushy billet', life was tough, and I was only sorry that I couldn't have done my bit for the Regiment which I loved for a longer period of time, but fate decided otherwise. A stray bit of shrapnel from a shell that wounded many others hit me in the centre of my forehead, and I have the scar to this day. It took off the majority of my nose, leaving only the bottom of my nostrils, my top lip over my bottom lip as there was nothing to hold it up, and the result was that I was unable to speak (the only time in my life I've been popular, one well known wag said). Most frightening of all, I was blind.

I have but very hazy recollections of coming and going mentally in the First Aid post and the hospital, except for hearing the voices of two Scots, one the Doctor Browning who had been on the destroyer *Kipling* that took me into Tobruk, and the other Abe Goodall who had been to Glasgow

Apologies for the rough state of this newspaper photograph: it is the only one still in existence showing the Ramb IV after its bombing en route to Alexandria with the author on board. Fortunately, such was the state of the author, he knew nothing about the bombing at the time!

Academy at the same time as brother Frank.

Morphia is a tremendous help in situations like the one which I was in: there was no hope of the surgeons in Tobruk dealing with my wound as it was a plastic surgery job. Yet Alexandria was days away as far as a patient was concerned: hospital ships only came in spasmodically since the route was extremely dangerous and higher command hoped that the number requiring evacuation would not be too great. So morphia was a super drug to keep us quiet until such time as we patients could get the treatment that our wounds required. As a result I recall nothing of the bombing of the *Ramb IV* on which I was transhipped from Tobruk to Alexandria. Except when in hospital on prescribed drugs I have never taken any (but have always enjoyed a libation of alcohol). However after those days of intense pain and the relief that morphia gave me, I can see only too well how some with all too little will power to say no get hooked, since under that drug's influence one can float on cloud nine! I little realised that had the *Ramb IV* gone down I would have been about to float in the Mediterranean, and that I, still blind and with morphia up to my sightless eyes would have known not one damned thing about it! But she made it back to Alexandria, and, as I have said on many occasions when reading the Bible lessons in church, 'Here endeth the second lesson'—this was the second time that the Jerries had tried to get rid of me and there was more to come!

Seven
NO. 8 GENERAL HOSPITAL, ALEXANDRIA

There were two British-staffed hospitals in Alexandria at that time, and I was destined for No. 8 General Hospital, as it had been chosen to be the base of the first Maxillo-facial Unit team to be sent to the Middle East. The team consisted of, first of all, a plastic surgeon, a Major Champion, a charming man who did his best in ten operations to restore my nose, but sadly for him, not me, he made little headway (or should I say noseway); Eric Dalling, a dental surgeon, who was an essential person in a team of this sort as nearly all, if not all, facial wounds have a tie-up with one's teeth; an anaesthetist for obvious reasons, and a sister whose full-time job was with the team.

They were extremely kind, and I know did all within their knowledge and experience to put on a new nose for me, but they lacked the experience of someone like Archie McIndoe whom I was so lucky to come under for my final fifteen operations. It was Eric Dalling who, bless his soul, told me 'Move heaven and earth to get to Archie McIndoe at East Grinstead, he's the tops'. I did move heaven and earth, or at least told a monumental lie, to get to East Grinstead, and found that Archie really was the tops! To give you an idea of how scared the Alexandria team were about putting a new nose back on me, here is what I heard when I was leaving No. 8 Hospital nine months later. The Yorkshire male orderly was getting me ready for despatch to a ship at Suez and said, with that lovely north country accent beloved of 'All Creatures Great and Small' fanatics, 'Ee, I remember when they were about to do the first operation on you, and it was Champion's first big one, so all the top brass was there. He'd told you he was going to make you look like Clark Gable, and no sooner were you under the anaesthetic than he said, in a whisper, to his team, "now where the 'ell do we bluidy start!"'

Anaesthetics then were the dreaded chloroform administered with a mask, and all too many of us were horribly sick after the operation. If I had the honour to present a prize to the person who did most to alleviate suffering I'd give it to the person who invented Pentathol, which Archie McIndoe's anaesthetist administered to me in East Grinstead Hospital. Jock Hunter was the anaesthetist, a great Scot, and he used to bet me I would never count up to twenty before I passed out, and I lost the bet every time.

Looking back after all those years, we all know war is ghastly, and yet for some unknown reason man has waged it for thousands of years. As armaments have become more and more sophisticated and fallen into hands that were much better off with spears, the wounds and human losses are ridiculously high, but at least the last world war saw a terrific breakthrough in surgery. My family tell me I'm too 'short in the fuse' when I castigate some of the follies of the young and say, 'I'll bet you were just as mad when you were young, Dad'. I didn't have the money they seem to have nowadays, and when it comes to motorbike madness, our old machines luckily could only do thirty miles per hour if we were lucky. But what I'm trying to get round to saying is that if the amount of experimental surgery that was tried on me, and sometimes came off and sometimes didn't, has helped anyone post-war, then I'm more than happy. There is no doubt in my mind that, at least as far as plastic surgery is concerned, thousands who have been treated since the last world war can thank the 'Guinea Pigs', not only the famous ones from the Queen Victoria Hospital sty but hundreds of others too. On these Guinea Pigs, very rightly, young surgeons were able to try out new ideas with no possibility of legal action should the operation go wrong which is one of the many curses we have to live with in this so-called 'with it' age!

The blindness passed away just before I was admitted to the hospital in Alexandria, for which to this day I say 'Thank God' literally. It was explained to me in hospital that although the optic nerve had been severed it can come together again, as can arteries, veins and skin when re-connected. Talking of skin, I was to remember in the period of my hospitalisation my lovely old Dad's remark, 'Wonderful stuff, skin, Ben, just look at a pregnant woman and see how extended it can become, and see how attractive she can be three months after the birth when it has contracted.' He ought to know, as he sired six of us! But staying in that hospital with not enough to do but roll bandages and wait for that magical hour when we were allowed to smoke, between 4 and 5 p.m., made one take an interest in what was being done for me and my pals. And as Dad had said, it is 'wonderful stuff, skin'. Nearly all of us who were having our wounds patched up by Champion were dependent on skin grafts, and grafting since those early forties has gone on from strength to strength.

The exceptions to those needing skin grafts were those with jaw injuries, and who should be among that lot but Jim Wynyard, the New Zealand All

Black against whom I had played, in what was to be my last game of rugby, when the Brits got thrashed by the New Zealand Division. (There's nothing new in this world!) Jim had his jaw broken by a bullet when patrolling in his 'Honey' tank in the desert as part of the New Zealand Division. What a division that was, and how right its Commander, General Freybergh, a V.C. of the First World War, was when he wouldn't allow his government to make up another division from New Zealand. He reckoned he wanted one cracking good division, and in my humble estimation he had the best in the Middle East. They were mainly volunteers, but what guts, what bravery and what dedication. Talking of which, in Jim Wynyard's case, he was one of four boys in his family, who had a small farm at Te Amawutu, and as one got killed in the 'Div Car' (short for Divisional Cavalry, as it was called in the First World War, now a light tank reconnaissance regiment) another went out and took his place, until after three had paid the supreme sacrifice their mother and father said, 'Enough is enough'. I went to visit their home in 1964, and the surviving brother was bitter that he had been ordered to stay and look after the farm. They are marvellous people, and to this day I buy New Zealand butter, yes, even ahead of Scottish which is pricing itself out of the market, because of what that wonderful division did for us in the war—though the war was no sooner finished than we gave them the heave-ho! But they are bred from resilient, mostly Scottish, stock and they have got rid of subsidies and have battled back to produce quality food which they sell world wide, how I wish we had had the foresight and guts in Scotland to do the same thing! You may well say I've strayed a long way from No. 8 General Hospital, Alexandria, but I haven't, because during the time we spent there Jim Wynyard was the catalyst of a lot of my thinking about farming, on topics like low input-low output, or Aberdeen Angus cattle and their use in New Zealand, whose Society I was to try to run for ten years as Chief Executive/Secretary in the Eighties.

We in the Maxillo-facial ward were all walking wounded, as by definition we had facial wounds, and the result was that between operations we were far too active by half! To deal with this Major Champion had teamed up with a group of ladies who wanted to help the war effort. Bear in mind that there were any amount of pro-Allied families in Egypt before the war: many were still there in 1941 and wanted to do their bit. So when we were not waiting for an operation or recovering from one, we were farmed out with a civilian family. This not only gave the hospital extra beds, which were badly needed as we were the nearest general hospital to the front line, but it made us as patients mentally more fit to face the next operation. As

The author with the incomparable Mrs B.—although American she was more British than are many Brits!

anyone who has waited for an operation will know, it's not exactly a time of rejoicing, and being in contact with people going about their everyday business and treating one normally did a lot for one's sanity.

The family who befriended Jim Wynyard and myself were the Brintons, who were Americans, although Mrs B., as we called her, was the greatest Anglophile and snob of all time. She was quite charming, a wonderful hostess and loved to name-drop. As one of a well-known American army family and an ex-girlfriend of the hero of the Philippines, General McArthur, she had entertained General Wavell and General Cunningham, the commanders on sea and land at that time in the Middle East. She was the greatest fun, big and busty, and 'the hostess with the mostest'. I don't think she had ever even boiled an egg in her life, as in the States her family had black servants, and in Egypt she depended on two super Sudanese, who fortunately stayed with her when she came to live in a London hotel where she died.

Judge Brinton, her husband, and she, his second wife, were as different as chalk from cheese. He was thin and wiry, a fitness fanatic and teetotaller, mean as get out and rather disparaging about the British war effort. I only wish he had been with me when I saw the pathetic efforts the Yanks made landing in North Africa! The judge was the senior in the mixed Court of Appeal in Egypt. Before the war it was a well-known fact that the Egyptians couldn't be trusted with this High Court, so two Americans, two British, two French, two Dutch etc. etc. judges were appointed, though for the duration the two Germans and two Italians were, shall we say, under house arrest! When I came back to Perthshire after the war a son of one of the British judges, one John Maxwell, heard that I knew Judge Brinton and told me he was his godson, but had never seen a sausage in the form of a present from him. To this I replied, 'Subject normal, he was a miserable old B.', and the word I had in mind was not Brinton. But no way could he diminish Mrs B.'s love of life and her wish to give hospitality to one and all who were aiding the war effort. Among the many whom I met at the Brintons was the Honourable Grizel Wolfe-Murray, a Black Watch officer's wife, daughter of the Earl of Glasgow, whom I was to meet later in not such happy circumstances.

Jim and I must have made a hit with the 'B.s', as every time we were released from hospital we were ordered to go to the B.s and who were we to complain? The judge was a great archaeologist and was also knowledgeable about desert flowers, and so that he could follow those two pursuits he had bought a house out in the desert at Burg el Arab. We used to go there from time to time, until suddenly Rommel made that brilliant burst down the desert to El Alamein.

I don't know what happened to the judge's house at Burg el Arab, but I did witness, and will never forget, what happened in Alexandria when the Egyptians thought the Germans and Italians were going to take the city. The story goes that the Axis forces were so sure they would do so that Mussolini had a special white charger sent to the front on which he was to ride victorious into Alexandria! As far as the people in the city were concerned all was mayhem. The residents, who knew which side their bread was buttered, had been tremendously pro-British, but as soon as they heard Rommel was at Alamein, which was, apart from the huge supply problem it caused, as good as at Alexandria's gates, they spat at us and tried to mug us if ever they had a crowd and we were single or in pairs.

Yes, things changed dramatically. Barclay's Bank had three storeys, and if you went up to the top you could see the lot. I've never seen such mayhem in my life, modern football hooligans are as angels to what I saw performed that day by the Egyptians in their efforts to withdraw their savings. Of course the fact that the participants wore a kind of cloak called 'galabeas', which resemble bell tents, added spectacularly to the scene. Jim and I were chased by a crowd when we tried to help a poor donkey that was being belaboured by its driver, and luckily we weren't far from the hospital so we got away. But worse was to follow. The one restaurateur in Alexandria who really was pro the Allies was Monsieur Pastroudi. When he heard the Jerries were at Alamein he knew that if they entered the city he was for the 'high jump', so he said that we, the hospital patients, could eat and drink free! What a day or two we had, until he realised that because of supply difficulties Rommel had been stopped in his tracks. I well remember the look on Jim's face when old Pastroudi said, 'Sorry, gentlemen, from tomorrow you pay, you drink too much'. He was looking at Jim: although he had a broken jaw, which meant it was wired up and he could only have liquids, to him, like the good New Zealander he was, that was 'nae bother'!

On the serious side, at that time most of the top personnel in the hospital were told they were to be evacuated over the canal and that volunteer nurses from Alexandria would take over the hospital. Looking back after all these years, how close we were to being snuffed out in the Middle East! And we might well have been, had not Russia come in and played such a significant part with their horrendous losses. The volunteer nurses were to be made up from the wives of the numerous civilian allied personnel. Alexandria pre-war was a very cosmopolitan town, and one could find just about every nationality that ever was there.

I'm not surprised, as even in war-time it had a lot going for it: none of the oppressive heat of Cairo in summer, excellent bathing in the Mediterranean, and first-class hotels and restaurants, where you were served by people who enjoyed serving you but were not servile. Being at the entrance of the Suez Canal, the place was really at the meeting point of three continents, so that it was always buzzing with gossip and intrigue.

There were some kenspeckle folk passed through the hospital during my stay. Randolph Churchill had a short visit and made himself most unpopular because he was always alluding to his father, though, as time was to tell, he was never a Winston. Lieutenant Colonel Roger Keyes came to call on fellow Black Watch officers who were wounded at the Tobruk break-out just after I was. His Victoria Cross, won in his gallant attempt to seize Rommel, is being auctioned in the week in which I write this.

The Earl of Cadogan, whom I now see at Perth Races, has reminded me that the first time he saw me I had two funnel-like objects up my nostrils in an effort to stop the nostrils shrinking as the surgical team tried to build up the nose itself. Champion's operations were based on a plan of building up the nose from the end of the nostrils, which were still intact but of course useless. Not only did he have the plastic funnels made, but also an artificial bridge of the nose which was mounted on a plate resembling a plate that holds one's false teeth on the upper jaw. 'The champ', as we called our plastic surgeon, would have been distressed to learn that when I got to the Queen Victoria Hospital, East Grinstead, Archie McIndoe took one look at all three objects, turned to his assistant, and said, 'Put this lot in the museum'. After a year depending on them, this left me feeling rather like a rugger player who has left his jock-strap behind!

Time would hang heavy on us when we were either being got ready for an operation or were recovering from one. However one job which we were given to do to help the nurses has stood me in good stead since the war, and that was rolling bandages. These were not the throw-away days to which we have become accustomed, everything was saved and re-used, so bandages were washed and re-washed and of course had to be re-rolled. The reason it was useful to me post-war is that my horse-mad wife and daughters have had to have their horses'/ponies' tails bandaged before they were loaded into the lorry or trailer taking them to the show or sale or whatever, and who better than this old man to roll the bandages!

The other thing we became adept at was killing flies, which are everywhere in the Middle East. Being honest at my time of life, I'd rather be a fly in Alexandria Hospital than, say, Crieff Cottage Hospital. Firstly, you'd be warmer, and secondly, you wouldn't have all the sprays etc. that we use in this country now, yes, and did use even then in the late forties and fifties. So we, the patients, used to lay bets with each other who could kill the most (or in some cases, any) flies! Gosh, they were wily: one had to come up behind them, and it took weeks in hospital, not days, to get into the super league of 'Fly Swatters'.

It is easy to overdo the brighter side of my spell in that Alexandria hospital, with those delightful stays at the Brintons between operations when one could swim in the 'Med' and be spoiled thoroughly, as all walking wounded were. I will take to my grave the memory of being invited to dine with the Yorkshire-born owner of the main English daily paper printed in Egypt, who had made a fortune. He had his own indoor swimming pool, which was unheard of in Britain in those far-off days, and every time one got out of the pool a great big Nubian came and rubbed one down. What impressed me most was (a) the huge size and softness of the bath towels and (b) the fact that each time they used a towel it was a new clean one! After my schoolboy experiences of bathing in the freezing waters (even in July or August) of Loch Earn, and drying oneself with something resembling a drying-up cloth for dishes, you can imagine that Coutts had never had it so good! But there was the other side to the coin: the dread of that next operation, and would the result be any better than the last? That feeling of despair that I'd never have a proper nose again, that I'd have to have the area exposed behind it douched out each day, oh, just every doubt that someone as restless as I am could conjure up about my future. And as I've said, we all hated the old anaesthetics of the chloroform mix which left you pretty sick. I wouldn't have been so restless had I felt that any progress was being made on my new 'proboscis', but all I seemed to be getting was bits of plastic to hold up what was left. Having said all that, I still retain the warmest regard and affection for that Number One Maxillo-facial Unit in Alexandria, who did their best for all of us who came under their care. I was to realise later, however, that they hadn't the experience or the expertise of some of the 'top brass'. But as I've described earlier, they learned so much that was to help plastic surgery post-war.

But time was running out for me as my blood count had run thin, and after ten operations in nine months they decided I should be sent home. It was a sad farewell to all the staff of No. 8 General Hospital who had been so kind to me, especially Sister Kitty McShane, Irish as you would imagine by her name and a very devout Catholic, who was dearly beloved by all of us under her tender care, as she was the tops. One of my regrets in a long life is that I never made contact with her after the war, as of the many Christians I've met in my life she would be in the top rank. She wrote a lovely letter to my parents, which sadly was mislaid, just saying that some (a very few I'm afraid) of the Christian ideals they had taught me had come out when I was a patient in her ward. Bless you, Kitty, I did try to help you and your nurses as much as I could, as you were very, very short-staffed, and it was the least we who were physically able could do to repay the horrendous hours you all did in those war years. I only wish the modern nurses, for whom I still have the greatest regard, could have seen the hours those girls in No. 8 General Hospital put in. Nursing is like being a small livestock farmer: it's a calling, the hours are long, there isn't much money, but oh! the pleasure one gets from doing a worthwhile job.

It was goodbye too to the Maxillo-facial Unit, who started off the reconstruction job on my 'Cyrano de Bergerac' nose as it was to be called before the final trimmings were carried out. Then it was goodbye to all my pals in hospital, not one of whom I've seen since, although I did visit Jim Wynyard's family in New Zealand in 1964, where he and his brothers are rightly local heroes. And finally, of course, I took leave of the Brintons, who had done so much to keep me sane for those nine months. Reading my very distant memories of fifty-four years ago it would be easy to think I'd had a whale of a time, but 'as time goes by', to quote a wonderful song, one remembers the good times and eradicates the bad ones! The visits to the Brintons helped eradicate the bad ones, and I will be forever in their debt.

However on 14 August I was put on a wonderfully captained and crewed ship, the P. & O. steamship *Stratheden*, bound, we thought, for home, with a very mixed bag of passengers. And off we set from Port Suez on what started as a picnic and finished as a disaster.

Eight
PORT SUEZ TO DURBAN AND FURTHER AND THE *LACONIA*

When I joined the P. & O. Liner *Stratheden* at Suez I was delighted to meet, once again, Grizel. Lady Grizel Wolfe-Murray, to give her her full title, was the Earl of Glasgow's daughter and wife of a major in the Black Watch. I had met her at the Brintons and she was immensely popular, a packet of fun. From the war-effort point of view she was a gem, as she was a great organiser of entertainment for the troops. One of the variety shows I saw in Alexandria, organised by Grizel, would not have been out of place amongst many professional shows I've seen since. Grizel, like many another Army wife pre-war, had followed and backed up her husband, Malcolm, and then got caught up in World War II. The reason she was coming home was that she was expecting a baby and wanted it to be born in Scotland, which sadly was not to be. A friend of hers, a Mrs Readman, had decided to stay on with her husband but was sending her fourteen-month-old baby, Sally, home with a highly experienced Nursing Sister called Doris ('Freckles') Hawkins because she, Mrs Readman, like many others, thought that Rommel, who had done so well already, might well over-run Egypt. So Grizel and Freckles were firm friends, and later shared a horrific experience, and until their dying days, in entirely different circumstances, were 'buddies' of mine because of that voyage.

As for the rest of the ship's complement, it would be hard to find a more mixed bunch. Because the Mediterranean was in the hands of the Axis we had women and children from Malta. Then there were walking wounded, of whom I was one. Time-expired servicemen were also aboard. I could never understand why, after a certain number of operations, R.A.F. pilots were sent back, as were certain Naval personnel, but not the old 'Brown Jobs', the Army. Although I must say we did have one or two ancient colonels, who were at least in their forties (strange how one's image of old age changes as one gets older). Then there were civilians who had been doing various jobs in the Middle East and were due for other duties at

'Grizel', Lady Grizel Wolfe-Murray

home. Among those was Bertie Miller, a fellow Scot, who was one of the civilian engineers on whom all the forces depend in war-time, and in his case he was training engineers in the R.A.F. This training was absolutely vital. For instance, what would I, trained in handling livestock, know about the finer points of a twenty-five pounder gun, or what would a fitter from a garage, recently joined up in the R.A.F., know about the intricacies of a Gloucester Gladiator or a Lysander, which is all we had early on in the Middle East! From the time we met, 'Jock' Miller, as I was to call him, and I were to be pals until his death in 1994. Sadly, because of differing ways of making a living after the war, we didn't see enough of each other.

Of the officers who were on board I was more than impressed with two. One was Squadron Leader Wells, who was to help Freckles and Grizel later on, and the other was Lieutenant Tillie, D.S.C. and bar, who had won his gong at Narvik and the bar in the Mediterranean. What I liked about them was their air of discipline which was to be a key factor in the rest of my story. Another officer was 'Cracker' Creedon, a major from the Border Regiment, who was also to become a pal. Life was all too easy on the *Stratheden* and it was not hard to imagine that one was having 'a cruise of a lifetime' as the holiday brochures would call it today! This it could have been had we not been transhipped at Durban. Most on board, and that certainly includes me, could not have afforded to travel on a boat of the *Stratheden*'s calibre and its service in those days.

When we got to Durban the skipper was given sealed orders which stated that we were all to be transhipped. When I was medically inspected, as we all were, the doctor said that they had a first-class plastic surgeons' team in South Africa and that I should wait there and be treated. Even now, after all those fifty-plus years, I wonder how I made the decision to say 'No, I'm sorry, I'm going back to the famous Archie McIndoe' (a complete fabrication!) I must say I was more than a bit tempted by his offer, as I love that country dearly and often wander what would have happened to my life had I decided to be operated on in South Africa.

But I had cast my die, and with all the rest who were going back to Britain we were put onto the Cunard liner the *Laconia*, built in 1922 by Swan Hunter, which had done twenty years' service when we boarded her in Durban. In her day she had been a well-known cruise ship and had had such celebrities as Noël Coward and his party travel to the West Indies on board. There are lovely photos in a book by Frederick Grossmith of the inglenook fireplace in the first-class smoking lounge and its famous garden lounge, complete with palm trees, and its sumptuous first-class dining room where I was to eat, though it didn't look the same in 1942 as when the original photograph was taken! Since those heady pre-war days of luxury cruising the old girl, like many another of our then super Merchant Navy fleet, had done her stuff for the war effort. It's sad looking back to think how many great ships built in Britain were lost in the war, never to be replaced, and how we now use ships from other countries with doubtful safety standards. However, talking of safety standards, at that time in the war the Merchant Navy was sorely pushed for man-power and had a 'pool' of seamen in Liverpool from which each ship had to draw some men to fill their crew requirements. As we were to find out all too many of them were not a patch an the Merchant Navy men who have made this old island of ours famous.

After a happy respite in Durban we got on board the *Laconia*, which we were to find out was hopelessly overcrowded with four hundred and sixty-three officers and crew, two hundred and eighty-six military personnel, eighty civilians who were mainly women and children, and one thousand, seven hundred and eighty-three Italian prisoners of war with their one hundred and three Polish guards: in all two thousand, seven hundred and twenty-five, which was way above the number the ship should have carried. Because of the overcrowding we, the officers, were getting vibes that all was not well down below. I must say their sleeping quarters were appalling, stuffy and claustrophobic, and I and Cracker Creedon made a point of visiting them with Colonel Baldwin who was O.C. Troops. We did our best to sort out some of the moans, but you'll always get some 'barrack-room law-yers' who have all the questions ready, like 'why, when we were in the front line, officers and rankers shared the hardships, but on this bloody ship you officers have a swell mess and bar etc., etc.?' Little did they know that the officers were not allowed any whisky, whereas the rankers were still getting their beer! Rumour had it that the whisky was only for those and such as those, the truth of which I know not!

Sadly, the Poles, who were guarding the Italians and were a grand bunch of disciplined soldiers, had a nasty slip up in that one of their number when cleaning his rifle let off a stray round of ammunition. This, of course, in an enclosed space, made one hell of a noise and confusion, and the order was given (by whom I know not once again) that each guard was only to have one round of ammo each. Whoever was responsible for this stupid order must be held responsible for some of the chaos that was to ensue later in our voyage. After hearing about this order 'Cracker' decided to form a volun-teer guard, as he was sure, and rightly as it turned out, that if we were torpedoed the Poles couldn't possibly stem the flood of one thousand, seven hundred and eighty Italians whose living conditions must have been absolutely appalling as our lot's were far from perfect! The voluntary part was the usual Army stuff, Cracker pointing to us individually and saying, 'You, you and you'. He had ascertained that I had a loaded revolver, so I was one of the 'volunteers'. Funnily enough, though I'm not a great collector of possessions, I liked that wee revolver. It was an Italian Beretta and it seemed, like a good shepherd's crook, to fit my hand, but the sharks are sharpening their teeth on it now! Cracker had worked out which gangways the Italians would burst from and assigned us to various ones.

Life passed slowly as we made our way up the West Coast of Africa, and as we were obviously zig-zagging we knew there must be U-Boats in the area. What worried most of us was that each evening the 'old lady' belched smoke from her single funnel, which we felt could be seen for miles, and we were proved to be right. Jock and I tried to exercise round the deck as much as we could, and in doing so I remember all too well (and I don't remember too much after fifty-three years!) that we thought the lifeboats looked a bit tatty and unserviced unlike those on the *Stratheden* and how right we were!

Grizel and Freckles were always great fun, as were Mrs Davidson and her daughter Molly. They had been evacuated from Malta, where Mrs Davidson's husband was Colonel of the Devons. Molly, then a teenager, is still with us and has managed to have two husbands since the *Laconia* days but she kept us all hopping then! There was a Church of Scotland minister on board, a Mr Copeland, one of the right sort, who organised ecumenical services, and as he had no voice he used to ask me to lead the singing for him, which I was more than glad to do. There was also a very kind Army doctor whose name escapes me. He was being returned home as he had some malady which he said was serious, but he wouldn't divulge what it was and he never complained. He it was who suggested, after seeing me 'hirpling' when I played deck quoits and finding that I had an ingrowing toenail, that I should have it removed while we were idling up the West African coast.

There was always a feeling of unease on the *Laconia*. She had seen better days, and although I never saw much of the crew I later found they were a divided lot. The old hands were the sort who made the 'Red Duster' (The Red Ensign) famous the world over, and some of them but for the war would have been retired. Then there were those from the Merchant Navy Pool in Liverpool, one of whom told me later he was damned if he was going into the forces as he wouldn't like the discipline or the grub and the pay was better in the Merchant Navy. Discipline was what was lacking, as we were to find out all too soon. On 9 September I went into the sick bay to have my toenail removed. I might say it was pure Coutts conceit that caused it to be an ingrowing toenail, as in Cairo I had a pair of winkle-pickers made to try to make my size twelve feet look smaller, and they completely compressed my toes. The ship's doctor was one Dr Purslow who was a topper. I can't remember much about my stay in the sick bay, except that I had the commonsense to take my haversack, my revolver and my Army greatcoat with me. The greatcoat was one of the last of the Cavalry type. Although short to allow one to ride a horse, it was wonderfully made and thick, with an inner lining in it, and I've no doubt it was my eventual lifesaver along with the odd drop of a liquid which we Scots hold dear and which is now drunk worldwide. My haversack was filled as ordered by Major George Munn on the outward voyage with a water bottle—how essential that was to be—hard tack, in the form in my case of chocolate, bandages (and I think iodine and an ointment of some sort), a whistle and a compass, and thank God I didn't need the latter as some did.

On Saturday night the minister came down to see me, as he always did, but I remember that occasion vividly as he said, 'Ben, will you make the service tomorrow?' I said of course I could, because it wasn't too far from the sick bay and I would return to have my toe dressed. We discussed the singing, and it's interesting that he chose 'Nearer my God to thee', the hymn sung just prior to the sinking of the Titanic—which, incidentally, although spoken of as the worst sinking ever etc., etc., didn't have as great a loss of life as we were to have, we lost two thousand!

I went back to my sick bay bunk on the Sunday evening, and had just finished my supper when the first torpedo struck. Before the Falklands war there were few people who knew where Ascension Island was situated, but ask any survivor of our ship and they'll know, as we were two hundred miles south of it at the time. The German U-Boat commander, of whom more later, said that thanks to the pall of smoke that the Laconia belched out each night we were served up on a plate for him. Suffice to say he put another tin fish into us, which sent my supper tray flying across the sickbay, put out all the lights, and moved everything that wasn't tied down. Firstly the boat tilted to the port (left) side, then, after the second torpedo, to the starboard, and this is how she lay for over half an hour. To this day I'm sure that if discipline had been properly administered and the Italians had been contained below for a bit longer and then regimented, many more could and should have been saved. Many ships were torpedoed during the war and had less time than ours to save their passengers, yet did so. But then we were hopelessly overloaded, with a mixture of personnel that no one in their right mind should have allowed. Ill guarded prisoners of war, women and children, civilians and all too many green Merchant Navy men is not a good cocktail mix!

Once the lights went out I put on my greatcoat over my pyjamas (silk and pinched from an Italian officer prisoner of war in Eritrea, or rather swopped for cigarettes, not too hot for the nights that were to follow!) Taking my haversack I was glad of my torch as I stumbled along a gangway that was at forty-five degrees. By the time I got to my pre-arranged station to stop the Italians it was already too late: they had, as 'Cracker' had feared, overwhelmed the Polish guards and were causing complete chaos on the boat deck. It was at this point that I realised how ill-disciplined the young seamen were, as they listened to no one. I have never seen such chaos in my life and never wish to see a sight like it again. When I saw the football disaster at Hillsborough on T.V. a shiver went down my spine, as it reminded me of the night of 12 September, 1942, on the *Laconia*.

I tried to contact Cracker but to no avail. I met Copeland, my minister, who had lost an eye and must have been in frightful pain, but he never complained and was doing his best to help women and children into the few serviceable lifeboats. You can imagine how difficult it is to launch lifeboats when a ship is at forty-five degrees to starboard, as the boats on that side are well away from the ship's side while those on the port side are literally stuck to the side. Freckles and Grizel were helped down a rope ladder, a most terrifying experience, and wee Sally was carried papoose-fashion by a New Zealander. They got into the last lifeboat to be launched, and it was no sooner pushed off than it was capsized by the weight of people hanging on to one side and wee Sally Readman was immediately drowned. I was to get to know her relations well when I came back to Scotland and reassured them she had no pain, but it's sad, sad, to think that she went with all her life in front of her, and had she lived she would be fifty-five this year! It was Squadron Leader Wells who had looked after Sally, Freckles and Grizel, as I with my toe in bandages could not move fast enough, but I helped carry some of the gear, which of course they lost, and which Freckles could have done with later on. It was when I was doing my best to help that my old pal Jock hove in sight. He was his usual cheery self, and the decent chap had been down to the sick bay to fetch me.

To add to the confusion the deck was strewn with rubbish that had come down when the ship was torpedoed: even the mainmast had ruptured, most was on the deck and you can imagine the tangle of struts, wires etc. that

The stern of the Laconia—and when the author looks at the size of the man in the foreground, he wonders fifty-four years on how he ever ventured down that swinging rope ladder!

caused. Because the mainmast was down no proper S.O.S. was sent out, and although the emergency set was used no vessel picked it up. When Jock and I looked over the side we couldn't believe what we saw: upturned lifeboats, rafts, mats, huge patches of oil, boxes, endless bodies—some swimming, but the red lights on their life jackets showing all too many floating face up, covered in oil—and, worst of all, sharks. I never realised that sharks abounded around the Equator, as I thought they were further south, but there were any amount about on that fateful night, and one heard harrowing stories from some of the survivors of friends being dragged under and of people being maimed and then dying a lingering death etc. Jock was wonderfully calm and was so good for me, as I'm well known for getting in a 'tizz'. He just said, 'I think it's time we got going, old man, we'll launch a raft from the stern as I don't like the look of that mess down there'. To reach the stern we had to go along one of the passage-ways, no easy matter when they were at forty-five degrees and most cabin doors had been forced open by the blast of the torpedoes. As we passed one, wonder of wonders, in my torch light what did we see but a row of spirit bottles, so we helped ourselves to one apiece. To my dying day I can't think what that cabin/bar was as we hadn't been allowed whisky for ages, and whether some clever dick had built up an Aladdin's cave or not doesn't matter, as it wasn't any use to him now, but it was certainly going to be some use to us in the days to come.

Jock got the raft and heaved it over the side having wisely tied its rope to the ship's rail. We then unhooked a rope ladder and he ordered me down first. I don't know how many readers have looked over the side of an ocean-going liner, but it's to me a terrifying distance to the sea and with my sore big toe it wasn't much fun descending the ladder! On the way down I heard Jock above me let out one large swear word, and he wasn't the average swearing Brit who prefaces everything with an 'F'. Some I heard on the *Laconia*, when talking about their photo taken with the *Hood* in Madeira called her a 'Battle-F—ing Ship'! Jock's expletive was mild compared with that, but his problem was vast as he'd broken his bottle of whisky! Once down on the raft our fight to save ourselves became real.

Nine
THE RAFT, A LIFEBOAT AND
LA GLOIRE

No sooner were we on the raft than the *Laconia* started ever so slowly to sink, bow first, and here were we with our raft still tied to her rail. But of course Jock had a knife—one that was extremely blunt—although I was ready to blow the rope off with my Beretta, about the last time I could have used it as, like everything on a raft, it got submerged in sea water. Jock sawed away for what seemed like hours, though I suppose it was only minutes, but he was just in time as the 'old lady' decided it was time to go. One had heard so much about the suction caused when a ship goes down that Jock and I pushed that raft away as hard as we could, and luckily we were both strong swimmers.

As the years go by, and it's now fifty-three of them gone, one forgets, probably luckily, some of the most ghastly parts of that night, but I will never forget the sight of that ship going to her death. There was something spectacular and yet eerie and also majestic in the manner in which she did it. Jock and I would be as near her in her dying moments as any of the survivors, and although the raft was drawn back some way towards where she sank, thank God, and I mean that literally, we were not sucked down. In the greatest of British maritime traditions Captain Sharp, having visited the chaos that should have been an orderly 'Abandon Ship', went down with her. As I've said earlier, as far as the complement of the ship was concerned someone needed their head looked at, but as far as the maintenance of the lifeboats was concerned, although a junior officer would be immediately responsible, sadly the 'buck' has to stop at the top.

The ship had no sooner disappeared than there was a ghastly explosion: whether it was the engine room or ammunition no one could ascertain, but all too many within close proximity were badly affected. Jock doubled up and was very, very sick and for the next hour or two I, for once, was the one in charge. Freckles, whom I was to see often after the war, got back trouble from it which lasted the rest of her life. Squadron Leader Wells, who had done such a super job was with Freckles at the time and he like Jock was doubled up with sickness. Lieutenant Tillie who, unbeknown to the rest of that lot, had done a sterling job on board with his naval draft, had waited until all the boats were away and then jumped from a ladder into the chaos below, only to break his arm which haemorrhaged. Of course nothing could be done when he too got the full force of the explosion, and sadly he died that night: but I for one will always remember a man who upheld the highest traditions of the senior service.

Meantime I was left paddling, not my 'lone canoe', but a raft with Jock on board. The ocean is vast, but vast, when you're on a raft; and the sea which from the deck of a liner had looked very calm was entirely different when one was on it! What I hadn't realised was that although we were near the Equator it was terribly cold at night, and pyjamas and a greatcoat are not the clothing I would have chosen for the next few days. Also it was strange how although there was that fantastic assembly of people in the water on the port side of the ship when Jock and I looked down—after all there were eight hundred to one thousand saved out of a possible three thousand plus— we saw not one single soul to begin with.

As that first night wore on we came in contact with others, but never a lifeboat. One I pulled onto the raft I shall never forget: he was a time expired Merchant Navy man, I think an engineer, who had come back to the service because of the war and was far from fit, and he was even worse clad for a raft than was I. He said he wouldn't be an encumbrance to us and he knew he wouldn't make home so he would slip off the raft before dawn. I'm a 'greetin' Geordie' at the best of times, but I'm proud to say I gave him a good swig of my whisky before he slipped over the side, which he did when I was having a cat nap. I only pray, and did then, that he drowned before the sharks got him. This all sounds ghastly now but this is what war was all about. I hope we never see it again, but sadly man has always wanted to fight (or hunt for prey which all too many townees can't understand).

Then there were the Italians, who, poor souls, were like rats in a trap in the bowels of the *Laconia* and were now free. Most were ill clad for a night on the Atlantic Ocean and all were pathetic in their will to live. We had one or two on our raft that night but every now and then one would drop off with a cry of 'Santa Maria' which cry we were to hear often in the ensuing days. Gosh! it was cold, that and every night that Jock and I were together. During that first night a submarine passed by, for all the world like a steel greyhound, a sinister, sleek shape, which looked like something man-made but made to destroy. All I can say is it gave me a funny feeling of fear, and yet we were to hear later that of all the sinkings in the war this was the one where the U-Boats came to the rescue, This was written up by Leonce Peillard in 1963 but Jock and I never saw any of it.

As that first night wore on we saw the odd Italian on a spar, flotsam ad nauseam, the odd oil slick, but not one lifeboat! We wondered how long it would be before we would be rescued. I had to 'ca' canny' with dispensing my precious drams. The sun came up next morning, and oh! how welcome to our cold aching limbs, and what should we see but a lifeboat right in front of us. Sadly, like all too many of the *Laconia's* lifeboats it had no food, water or blankets on board, and it had a large hole in it, caused, I would think, by the torpedo blast or by banging against the port side of the ship when being lowered. But as it had buoyancy tanks it still had its gunwales above the surface, and compared with a raft it would mean travelling de luxe, as one could walk in it even if up to one's ankles, or higher, in salt water. When I left the hospital in Alexandria they said to me to be sure and give my nose plenty of saline solution! but I don't think they meant the whole of the Atlantic Ocean (plus some oil on that first night).

On board this submerged lifeboat we found the ship's second officer, one Rose, who was in charge of nine British and six Italians, all of whom had to bale non-stop to keep the boat just half full of water. We did try to block the gap with some gear from the locker, but we knew we were fighting a losing battle, as after Rose had hoisted a makeshift sail the boat wouldn't sail as he wanted it to because of the weight of water and personnel. What was annoying was that we could see other lifeboats, but we seemed to be drifting away from them instead of sailing to them. Rose was adamant we had to lighten the boat's load. As we were baling as hard as we were physically able, with the one and only small bucket, the only way to lighten her was to put the Italians—who were useless at baling, the poor devils were half starved—onto the raft that Jock and I had come on. We had tied this to the lifeboat 'just for fear', as my old shepherd Robbie McHardy used to say if he was afraid things would go wrong. Rose fed them first with the small amount of rations available, and he then gave me the task, with not one word of Italian, of ushering them onto the raft. The awful thing about war is that one has to look after oneself first. Although I feel pangs of conscience about agreeing with Rose to put them on the raft, firstly we had fed them, which we didn't have to do, secondly, they were dry on the raft and we were very, very wet and thirdly, they couldn't bale. But I still felt more than a pang of conscience in the morning when only one out of the six was still there.

One of the few lifeboats that were launched from the Laconia, *and, as one can see, it is hopelessly overloaded. The picture was taken by a German from one of the U-boats*

Strange how one always thinks of the Equator as being hot, but it's the cold nights I remember, and also the fact that wading around in sea water with the sun blazing through it gave one elephantiasis. At the best of times I have a tender skin, and my family laugh at me when we go on holiday somewhere 'in the sun' and I stick to the shade, but if they had seen the mess I was in after those five days on a raft and a lifeboat they would see why.

Those other boats we had seen on the horizon and which Rose assured Jock and me had been told to await a rescue vessel, were nowhere to be seen when dawn broke, and Rose was determined that we should set sail for land. This, in a very dicky boat, seemed daft to me, and in fact Jack and I were rather glad we had 'our' raft in tow. I think situations such as the one we were in make one light-headed, as when Jock and I discussed it with Rose the next day he agreed the idea was not on. Our only hope was to meet up with other lifeboats, as he assured us that a submarine commander had said we were to be rescued at a certain rendezvous (not too easy to find without a proper compass in the middle of the Atlantic).

I will always remember that glaring sun reflecting through the water, and the pain, not the pleasure, it gave one. I remember how Jock and I used to dowse each other when we were on baling duty, and Jock laughing and saying, 'Do you think the surgeon in Alexandria reckons you've had enough saline solution today?' Then those awful nights when the wind whipped through you, and I thanked the Almighty for my greatcoat which the poor Italians hadn't got. Then there was nowhere to lie down, as the water kept rising, so one never really slept. Two books have been written since the *Laconia* sinking, and although neither author consulted me they bang an about my bad toe, but were both kind enough to say I remained cheery. What they didn't know was that with nothing to stop the water, as I had no nose or at least no top half to it, had I been immersed or pulled under the surface as were many by those trying to get onto rafts or lifeboats, I would have been a 'goner'.

We carried on in our half-submerged lifeboat for three days, when suddenly one morning we came on another lifeboat completely overcrowded. I think there were fifty-five in it instead of the twenty-four which it should have had. This lifeboat was in first-class condition and had on board many of the remaining senior officers, among them Colonel Baldwin who was O.C. troops on the *Laconia,* and also three or four of her officers. To allow us on board they made the Italians swop places with us, and was I glad to get my swollen legs into that dry boat. For the first time almost since leaving the *Stratheden* there was some real sense of discipline, as between the Colonel and the ship's officers things were under control. They had set a sail but were going to wait another day for the promised rescue. They were extremely strict with the food and water ration and oh! how we yearned for the latter. Jock and I always had our wee tot of whisky when it was dark, it didn't do much for our thirst but it did a hell of a lot of good for our morale!

On the fifth day after the sinking as the sun was rising, 'Glory be', there was a ship bearing down on us—and it was 'Glory be' all right as she was *La Gloire,* a French cruiser. She had been sent out from Dakar on the instructions of Admiral Doenitz when the U–Boat commander had signalled to shore that he had torpedoed a liner on which were Italian prisoners of war and women and children. Seven boats in all were picked up by *La Gloire* at the rendezvous spot. Not many, considering the thirty-two lifeboats that were originally on the *Laconia,* but there were more survivors to be picked up that had made their way to *La Gloire* by other means.

Strange how, after being tossed around in rafts, lifeboats etc. in what was after all the middle of the Eastern Atlantic, and being some nine hundred miles from land, how smooth we thought it looked when the cruiser came up to us, but we were to find out how wrong we were when the lifeboat was actually alongside as we pitched and tossed like a cork. One member of our party, Wing Commander Mears, was struck so forcibly by the cruiser's stabilisers that he sustained multiple damage to his rib-cage, including six broken ribs. The French matelots were super and threw down ropes and boarding nets. However I just couldn't start to climb up them as my legs were useless, but they got me up. Imagine our joy to be welcomed by coffee and brandy, once again served by the matelots.

Sadly the officers were not of the same mind—whether it was shades of our navy hammering them in Mers-el-Kebir when the French navy wouldn't make up their mind whether they would remain as an ally or go with the Vichy lot, and then decided to join the Vichy lot, or maybe it stemmed from Trafalgar, I know not—but anti-British the officers were all the time we were on board their ship. My memory fades as the years go on apace, but I will never forget, or forgive, a young French naval officer booting me up the backside as I crawled from our crowded quarters to the only available loo, as with my swollen legs I couldn't walk. The next time I wanted to go, and because of dehydration it was days after, I peed where I lay! There's an ingrown loathing of the Brits among certain of the French which I was to come across later in my epic journey home.

As we came to physically and mentally things started to take shape. Colonel Baldwin, the sort of whom anyone who served in the Army should be proud, took charge and made a roster of the thirty-six British and Polish officers. These were to see that the survivors were properly controlled, as instead of being thankful that they were saved, some, believe it or not, were moaning about being prisoners and only getting two meals a day (at 11.30 a.m. and 6 p.m.) As these were hot compared with the Horlicks tablet and hard tack they had had on the lifeboats, what were they moaning about? But 'there's nowt queerer than folk' as the Geordies say.

We had yet another burial service when Third Engineer Jackson was committed to the deep, and I was meant to lead the singing but was blubbering like a bairn. We were burying this man at the most magical time of day on the Atlantic, when the sun is going over the skyline and a green ball appears for a few seconds before night falls. If I hadn't been so lucky and had to die after the sinking, that's when and how I would like to have gone, and certainly not to the sharks!

The cruiser went back to Dakar to get its orders, which were to re-fuel and re-victual as we were to be taken round to Casablanca. Strange how the fortunes of war can alter by the day, as only the day before we boarded the cruiser we had been ordering the Italians about, but now they as allies of the Vichy French were, as the French matelots said, 'simply insufferable, insolent and arrogant'.

During our time on *La Gloire* I was more than sorry for the women and children. There is no room in a fighting ship for hundreds of ill-clad and illnourished extras. But the women were marvellous, clad all too often in one thin dress which was completely useless for keeping out the chill of an Atlantic wind. But they still found time to organise games for the children, whom I sadly never got to know. But one thing I do remember was the meeting up of Mrs Davidson and her daughter Molly, who had come to *La Gloire* by entirely different routes. They were the people who were able to tell me that life for a woman on a ship-of-war, among a lot of men speaking another language, was not easy. But again Colonel Baldwin had been a wonderful mediator between the women and the crew.

It would seem from later records that the French (Vichy and Pro-Axis in this case) were sure that the Allied landing in Africa, or at least part of it, would happen there, i.e. Dakar, and no way did they want to have us around. So it was off with us to Casablanca, a town of which I was to see quite a bit—though not, sadly, Rick's Bar, immortalised by that wonderful song 'As Time Goes By' from the Humphrey Bogart film, which everyone in the world must know although they have never seen the town! For once the American film people got it right, as when we were there the whole place was full of intrigue, and the Germans were controlling everything although on the surface not wanting to be seen doing so. But as always my pen pushes me on, and we weren't yet in Casablanca.

When we got there the Italians, as allies of the Vichy French, went down the gangway first, and we, the British, were last. Colonel Baldwin, typically army style, formed us British up in ranks, and a pretty poor lot of specimens we looked. He said 'Vive La France!' and called for three cheers for the French, which we followed with the naval Hip, Hip, Hooray! The nice sequel to this was that the matelots waved their sailors' bonnets with their red pom-poms on them, and cheered in return, but the officers turned their backs.

And so we had arrived in North Africa, which for me was to be the start of another saga on my journey home. Of those who began the voyage on the *Laconia,* some had arrived on *La Gloire* by completely different means, two boats made land and two thousand plus passengers were lost in various ways—drowned on the sinking ship or mauled afterwards by sharks, perished from thirst or exposure or just because the will to live wasn't there. Whatever the causes, with a bit of better planning, forethought and most of all discipline, many more should have been saved.

Ten
HOW OTHERS GOT (OR DIDN'T GET) TO *LA GLOIRE*

Mrs Davidson, whom I've already mentioned, with her teenage daughter Molly, were being evacuated from Malta where Mrs Davidson's husband was Colonel of the Devon Regiment. Malta had had that terrible pounding and strafing which earned it the George Cross, so that the Davidsons had had their fill of the war and its terrors before we were torpedoed. Mrs 'D' was what my father used to call 'a card', i.e. a character. One of the old school, she was used to army discipline and gravitated to the likes of Major 'Cracker' Creedon, who formed our volunteer guard on the ship, and other service officers like Colonel Baldwin, John Tillie and myself. In fact before my big toe gave me trouble I had the odd dance with her, although I thought at the time she had one foot in the grave, she was forty-three! She enjoyed her odd spot of gin and a fag, everyone smoked in war time. She was wonderfully outspoken and I'm glad that when she eventually made land she managed to keep a diary (which was typical of her, as keeping a diary in wartime was strictly forbidden!) as some of her 'mots justes' were classics.

When the first torpedo had struck, Mrs Davidson was thrown across the lounge. As it was evening she was wearing a thin silk dress and her shoes were high-heeled sandals, not the best sort of attire for the next few days she was to experience. She and Molly, like everyone else on board, made for the boat decks only to encounter the total chaos I have already described. The cry of 'Boat Stations' was heard everywhere, followed by 'Abandon Ship'. The latter order was harder to obey than it should have been. The Davidsons had their lifebelts put on by 'Dusty' and 'Joss', two of their R.A.F. pals. Then Cracker strolled up as if nothing unusual was happening and said, 'we'll need to find places for you two in a boat'. What a great influence he had on us all during that incident and also later. I remember he, Mrs Davidson and I discussing the night of the sinking when we met up later on, and all agreeing one of the things that disgusted us most was seeing boats with some members of the crew and some prisoners of war in them being cast off half empty, and women and children still on the boat deck. Cracker urged the Davidsons on, pushing them towards a rope ladder with Mrs Davidson saying, 'You first, Molly,' and Molly replying, 'No, you mummy'. Anyway, Molly led the way and eventually got to the bottom, only to be hit on the head, why or with what she knew not, but she saw stars and landed into a boat already crammed full and badly manned, as those on the oars had obviously never competed at the Henley Regatta!

Meantime 'Mummy' was getting into all sorts of trouble on the rope ladder, as someone had kindly lent her an overcoat to put over her silk dress, and its belt and the lifebelt cords got mixed up. But the Major got her sorted out and in fear and trepidation she edged down the ladder. At the bottom there was no boat, so she jumped into the muck that was once a clean sea. Personally, looking back, it was the oil, the floating corpses, and the sharks that still haunt me, and that's what Mrs Davidson was in amongst. But she was luckier than some, as a lifeboat nearby collided with her and she grabbed the painter and was pulled on board. In her diary she talks about the haunting cry of the Italian prisoners who could be heard all night crying 'Aiuto! Aiuto!' whereas our Italians were always crying, 'Santa Maria!' Like us all she notes how she could never get over the sight of the floating corpses, and especially that of John Tillie, dearly respected and beloved by all, floating head up in his Mae West life-jacket.

She is wonderfully scathing about a certain R.A.F. officer, 'one of those pen-pushing wallahs, Ben, being sent home because he was no bloody good'. This officer had the misfortune to be in charge of Mrs Davidson's over-crowded boat and I'll bet she gave him stick. Also in the boat was a ranker's wife who had lost a child and kept chiding Mrs Davidson for not being sympathetic enough, little realising how typically stoic she was being in not bemoaning her own daughter Molly's loss, as no trace of her was recorded among the few lifeboats that were in hailing distance of each other.

Meantime among some of the other lifeboats a U-boat appeared, and the captain, in perfect English, said over a loud hailer, 'Are there any wounded among the Italians, as I'll take them on board', and then following that, 'I am sorry for you but your ship was armed as an auxiliary cruiser, you will surely be rescued as wireless messages were sent and I shall not attack rescue ships'. This captain turned out to be Lt. Commander Werner Hartenstein, commander of the U-156 which had torpedoed the *Laconia*. He was left in a terrible dilemma when he found that there were one thousand, eight hundred prisoners of war plus women and children on board the ship he had just torpedoed. He had wirelessed Admiral Doenitz as to what he should do, as there was controversy in the German high command as to whether U-boats should take survivors on board or not, and it is chronicled that Hitler had ordered that 'if foreign seamen could not be taken as prisoners, which in most cases is not possible, U-boats were to surface after torpedoing and shoot up the lifeboats.' Luckily for the *Laconia* survivors, myself included, Hartenstein and his fellow U-boat Commanders plus their boss Doenitz were made of kinder material, and did a wonderful rescue operation, although little did we realise then that the '*Laconia* Incident' was to figure large in the Nuremberg War Crime Trials.

U-156 was but one of a pack called the 'Polar Bears', and Hartenstein signalled to the others to rendezvous with him. Mrs Davidson (after days in the lifeboat) was hauled onto the U-507 commanded by Commander Schacht. Like us all she couldn't walk because of the effect of sun and salt water. Her 'bête noir', the R.A.F. officer, and the moaning woman were among the twenty-four British and thirty-one Italians taken on board, and the total was some one hundred plus. Looking back after all these years the three submarine commanders were taking one helluva risk, a very real one as it was to turn out, by having all those survivors on board. Their orders were only to take on as many extra personnel as would still allow them to dive. In the case of Schacht's submarine, the U-507, he had one hundred and fifty-three survivors, but thanks to the chief engineer Peter Achfeldt they did it most successfully, what an achievement.

The 507 took eight lifeboats in tow and Mrs Davidson, the R.A.F. officer and the moaner were kept on board the U-boat. However, all in the lifeboats had been fed and watered—the latter being the more important, as without liquid one couldn't even swallow the Horlicks tablets or the chocolate, far less the hard tack biscuits that should have been in every lifeboat. As it was, I never met one survivor who could truthfully say that his or her lifeboat had been properly victualled and many said theirs had nothing and no water! A disgrace, and quite the worst example of incompetence in the whole sad affair. However the Germans seemed to eat well, with porridge, black bread from tins, Norwegian butter, strong coffee and milk from the south of France and German preserves, all this for breakfast; and for lunch macaroni and tomato, meat and vegetables from tins. Then there were sardines, bacon and sausages for supper and plenty of water, as they had a de-salinator which took the salt out of the salt water. But the great thing about Dorothy Davidson's account of the Germans on that submarine was that they were so kind and understanding, and were sharing all this grub with their enemies, giving the women ointment for their sunburn and escorting them around the sub 'in case they were molested by the Italians'. The Italians, who after all were still their allies, were made to clean up! It just shows how wrong propaganda can be, as we had been taught how terrible the Germans were, and most occupants of the lifeboats were terrified when the U-boats came alongside to get them collected up (for all the world like sheep dogs with a flock of sheep) so that they would be at the rendezvous point for *La Gloire*.

Just shows there are good and bad in every country. None of those who were taken on board from the three lifeboats ever saw a swastika or heard 'Heil Hitler' uttered, and there was but one photo of Hitler. Sadly, all three commanders of the U-boats did such a super job not knowing how their higher command would view their action, and also in the knowledge they could be bombed as one in fact was. Sadly, as I say, they all eventually paid the supreme sacrifice. As Freckles Hawkins was to say in the Foreword to her book *Atlantic Torpedo*, 'Even in the midst of war one must recognise gratefully the humanity shown to us survivors by the personnel of the German submarine that picked us up'. Contrast the U-boat commanders' behaviour with that of those in charge of Belsen: the release of those pitiful skeletons fifty years ago is by chance being commemorated on this very day as I pen this chapter! Dorothy Davidson's remarks about the food on the submarine compared with that on the French cruiser were typical of her. She said, 'The best of French cooking may be the tops but their plain cooking is bad, messy and dirty, whereas the German plain food was clean and good.'

Then she said to me, 'But I was nearly reduced to a liquid diet, as when I was pulled into that first lifeboat I nearly lost my teeth'. Dear Dorothy, if you'd been confined to a diet of the odd spot of gin would you have objected? But more serious was Freckles' loss of her specs. These were pretty strong, but for the next twenty seven days she wouldn't need them and in due course I'll explain why. None of the ladies ever told me how they managed to deal with 'the little duties we have to do each day', to quote a line from a hymn that father, a Church of Scotland minister, could never use because the Manse pew used to collapse in laughter! It must have been especially embarrassing for 'Freckles' as she, the topper that she was, had lived a very upright, celibate and Christian life, in fact looking back she was one of the most outstanding Christians I've ever met. Dorothy D.'s observations of the sanitation on *La Gloire* were typical of her: 'French sanitation is most odd'.

Another among the survivors was Buckingham, who had been third officer on the *Laconia* and was just about the last man to leave her, as she was actually going down when he got off her. He survived the first night by actually hanging on to a floating corpse! He must have been a fantastic swimmer, as he saw a lifeboat in the distance and swam for an hour to get to it. When he got to it he found it was standing room only, with Dr Purslow, the ship's doctor, in charge. There were dozens of Italians hanging on to the gunwales, the cause of most of the capsized lifeboats on the night of the sinking. He heard from the Doctor that there was another lifeboat with few in it not far off, and Buckingham swam for nearly another hour to that, what a man, and then he went back to Purslow's boat to get some of the hangers-on persuaded to come to his boat.

If only there had been more Buckinghams as officers on the *Laconia* there could have been less carnage. But having said that, I wonder how he felt when he took charge of four lifeboats, and knew that land was nine hundred miles away and not one lifeboat had its full stock of food, water, sails, rockets, sea anchor, torch batteries etc., etc. Buckingham's four boats were taken in tow by the U-507, and he never understood how the U-boat commander knew he was an officer as he only wore a shirt and shorts, but he did. When the rest were released back to their lifeboats, Buckingham was kept as a prisoner of war in case he had seen anything on board the U-boat that might be of interest to British Intelligence, so the poor chap finished his war in a German P.O.W. Camp.

Meantime Molly, Dorothy's daughter, was being looked after on another submarine and was one of nine women who with three children and one hundred and forty-two Italians were then put on board the French destroyer *Annamite*. To tranship that number it took one small boat twenty-five journeys! All too many had shark bites, heels taken off, tibia bones showing, you name it, the sick were really sick, but the French did their very best with limited facilities. What a funny mix-up that whole sinking was. Firstly a British liner sunk by a U-boat who treated the survivors wonderfully, then the Italians who were their allies being made to clean the submarine! Secondly the Vichy French, who were meant to be allies of Germans and Italians, treated the Italians like scum. The *Annamite* commander told Molly Davidson that his wife lived in Vichy where she was being badly treated by the Germans, so he hated them and was himself pro-British, but had to do what he was told. He and all his crew were kindness itself to Brits and Italians alike and were amazed that the U-boats hadn't machine-gunned the former, such was the propaganda.

Meantime, while the submarines were towing the lifeboats to the rendezvous, and although Hartenstein's submarine had a Red Cross prominently displayed, an American Liberator bomber flew over dropping four depth charges. Two hit one of the lifeboats in tow and killed the occupants and the other two lifted the U-boat out of the water and severely damaged her. It was many years after the end of the war that the mystery of the bombing was unfolded. It seems the Americans had been building an airfield on Ascension Island to give them a base close to Africa for their impending invasion, and they were determined to keep it as secret as possible. Of course like many another fighting unit they had their 'trigger happy' members who would let fly at any target. The action was to have far-reaching consequences, not only for the *Laconia* survivors but for all future survivors of ships, as Doenitz was to say 'enough is enough, in future we save no one'.

As a result the survivors were ordered back to their lifeboats from the comparative comfort of the U-boats. One has to feel sorry for all those who were not good swimmers, facing, yet again, 'the cruel sea' with its waves, sharks and jellyfish. Many of us had jellyfish bites and damned sore they were. No one dreaded it more than Freckles Hawkins, who was on her own admission a poor swimmer. With her fair skin and auburn hair she had appreciated the ointment for her sunburn, and the care and attention she and the other women had received from the U-boat crew.

She it was who told me many months later how my padre friend Copeland, with an eye literally hanging out, but never complaining, carried out a burial service on the submarine and later felt he was being an encumbrance to the rest in the lifeboat, so one night he just slipped overboard. After hearing about this I wrote to his widow saying what a super job he had done, and like Captain Oates in Captain Scott's South Pole expedition he had gone out, Oates to the snow and Copeland into the sea, in order that others could live. Imagine my amazement when I got a very stuffy letter back saying Oates (who was a boyhood hero of mine) had committed suicide and was I comparing her husband with him? That letter seared me and I didn't write any more to relatives of those we lost.

Freckles and Grizel were towed for nigh on an hour by Squadron Leader Wells, another fine swimmer, to the nearest lifeboat, but he did not get into it and sadly died ten days later. I wonder if that American pilot realised that his completely uncalled-for action caused umpteen deaths, as apart from the sixty-six Brits and two Poles in this lifeboat which was to head for land, all the rest perished when help was so near at hand. This lifeboat was commanded by the ship's doctor, Purslow, who was called the Navigating Doctor as he had done a bit of sailing pre-war. He had the stores checked over, and it was the old story, all too much was missing including the medicine chest,

Doris Hawkins O.B.E., one of the finest Christians it's been my pleasure to know, and one of the few who came through an historic 27-day voyage in a lifeboat and survived, thanks to her faith

rockets and flares and the sail, which they were going to need desperately as they didn't know where they were to rendezvous or whether the Vichy French would turn up or not. Just imagine the thought of setting out for land (estimates of the distance varied between six hundred and nine hundred miles) in a leaking thirty-foot wooden lifeboat with sixty-eight people on board, insufficient water and food and no sail! Freckles' account of the voyage, *Atlantic Torpedo*, written in 1943 (price one old shilling!), is one of the epic stories of the war. Sixty-eight of them started off, and their journey finished twenty-seven days later, but only sixteen survived and she was the only woman. She gave me a copy of her book, and full permission to use any of it should I write of my own experiences, and we used to meet from time to time. The last time I saw her she was happily retired on the Sussex coast, but sadly she slipped away a couple of years ago. She was a very brave and upright Christian woman with a great sense of humour.

With no sail they rigged a tarpaulin to an oar. Like all too many of the lifeboats, theirs leaked and had to be baled regularly. They only had fifteen gallons of water for sixty-eight people. They started off rowing, but after a few days they were too weak and took turn about on the tiller. Their food ration was four Horlicks tablets and three pieces of chocolate (1½" x ¾" x ¼") and no water in the morning. Evening, two ships' biscuits (very dry and hard and which soon they couldn't swallow because of lack of saliva), one teaspoonful of pemmican and but two ounces of water, which they swilled round their mouths and tried to make it last.

After a few nights some couldn't take the pressure, and started to drink sea water and went mad and jumped overboard. This made room for Freckles and Grizel to lie together behind the makeshift mast, but Grizel was fading fast and talked constantly of home and family. Knowing that it was dark from 6.30 p.m. to 6 a.m. and very cold at night, and then blazing hot all day and with no shelter, I having experienced it for but five days still wonder how the sixteen made land. The sharks followed them all the way with the uncanny knowledge that yet another member of that boat would soon be destined to be buried at sea. One of the party, Billy Henderson, was 'immense'—he made a new rudder, worked for the comfort of all, never spared himself and took the worst shifts at pumping, having organised a rota for the shifts. He it was who made a notice-board on which he wrote 'S.O.S. water', which was to be more than useful near the end of their voyage. Sadly Billy was not to be one of the fortunate sixteen who made land, but those who did so remember him with gratitude.

After eight days Grizel just faded away, and Freckles was left the sole woman survivor for a further nineteen days of pure hell. As I've said, she'd already lost her specs, and her eyes discharged pus as the light was so strong. All their pores closed up completely as they hadn't enough moisture in their bodies to perspire. All had salt-water sores, septic fingers and/or boils. Dr Purslow and Freckles were constantly opening septic fingers and toes with an old pen-knife cleansed in salt water—a bit different to the sterilization procedures we see in the medical T.V. shows that have become so popular recently! The lack of water was the worst of their many, many problems, as Freckles told me it took her an hour to swallow her teaspoonful of pemmican, which she was determined to do as she knew from her nursing training of its high food value. The chocolate dissolved easily, but of course the supplies ran out! If only there had been some fishing tackle on board they would have saved many more, as one flying fish landed in the boat and even among the number it had to be divided it gave them fresh heart. Tins of salt water were poured over them every day which seemed to be absorbed through the skin. They kept having occasions of terrific optimism, a plane would be heard, a boat would be sighted, but no one came to their rescue and they were getting fewer and weaker by the day. On the nineteenth day Dr Purslow, who had been such a magnificent leader and example to others, decided as he had blood poisoning and would be a danger to the rest that he must go, and Freckles saw him over the side saying the immortal words, 'Greater love hath no man than this, that a man lay down his life for his friends'.

Into their third week of purgatory and the water ration was finishing and no one could eat the dry food when the water ran out. Freckles, the great Christian she was, got the few remaining to get down on their knees and pray, and as she said to me many years later, 'There are those who scoff at the power of prayer, but next day we had a torrential downpour lasting six hours!' They filled every container they could find, including the makeshift sail which coloured the water yellow, but 'wot the 'ell', it was blessed, life-giving water. After this they were all able to eat the Horlicks tablets and ship's biscuits. If only it had come sooner so many more would have been saved. All the officers had gone. After the rain they started to see birds and knew they must be close to land. When they eventually made a landing they didn't realise how lucky they had been, as they beached on the one bit of sand in the middle of miles of rocky coast line. Before they made land, which took three days from the time they saw the first birds, an aeroplane had circled over them and they had displayed Billy's notice with 'S.O.S. water' written on it. Back came the aeroplane and dropped a lifejacket right beside the lifeboat, and on the lifejacket was written 'O.K. help coming, you are sixty miles south of Monrovia'. As Freckles said to me, 'I'll bet you didn't know where Monrovia was, Ben, any more than we did'. How right she was.

There were many more trials and tribulations, the worst being taken home from Monrovia, after six weeks in hospital, on the sister ship of the *Laconia* and unescorted! This was in submarine-infested seas and with all of three thousand miles to sail, but she made it. Freckles, those of us who knew you, admired you and salute you not only for what you came through with what Churchill would have called the 'bulldog spirit', but for the Christian example you showed to all, both before and after the torpedoing. I am only sad you're not alive to read what I've written.

And so when this boat eventually made land after their horrendous experiences and losses, the *Laconia* episode was a closed book, or so those of us survivors thought, until the Nuremberg War Trials when the sinking became known as 'the *Laconia* order'.

Eleven
CASABLANCA

Molly Davidson has refreshed my memory about our arrival at Casablanca. We were loaded into coaches and taken on a two to three hour drive to a camp called Medouna, which was a collection of mud huts, some joined together, and guarded with sentries who had pre-First World War rifles! We had all taken our life jackets with us, I can't think why, but they were mighty useful as pillows and once again we were made to sleep on the bare boards of a big hut. They say it's good for one's back to sleep on a hard surface, so no survivor of the *Laconia* should ever suffer again from a bad back! Molly remembers the Commandant as a retired Foreign Legion Colonel who always had two gorgeous Moroccan girls in tow. (Old age must be creeping up on me as I can't remember them, how remiss.)

The ladies from the *Laconia* very rightly wanted better, more private quarters than the vast hall in which they were dumped, and got 'tukuls', like those I'd had in the Sudan, assigned to them. The 'loos' were as always pretty awful, but a good looking Arab whom Molly christened 'Clarence the Cesspit' kept them fairly clean and one had to get there first thing in the morning or the stench was unbearable.

I hadn't appreciated until I got Molly's account how many other nationalities there were in that camp. There were Austrians, Czechs and other Europeans who had fled the Reich. There was a Swedish woman, and as Sweden was neutral she was allowed to go shopping each weekend. There was a Spanish chemist who saved Molly's arm by getting rid of a nasty carbuncle. I often wonder now how little the people at home, living on an island, realised what was happening in Europe when Hitler launched his attacks on Czechoslovakia, Poland, France etc. and the flotsam that washed up in places like Casablanca as a result.

The food was quite ghastly, watery stew and hard bread: there was wine but it was more like vinegar! As always a black-market flourished, and dear Mrs D., like all of her generation, would not be parted from her handbag throughout our ordeal so she had a wee bit to spend. The Swedish lady, greatly daring, went into the American Embassy and asked to see the Ambassador. When he was told that there were British being held by the Vichy French, officially as 'Internees de Guerre', but for all intents and purposes as prisoners of war, he was furious. Furious, because as the Yanks were, up until a month later, neutral, he was responsible for British affairs and should have been told of our plight. So annoyed was he that he threatened to stop the shipments of food which the Moroccans were receiving, since the Nazis were taking everything they could grow in Morocco and shipping it to France. The effect of the Swedish lady's visit to the Embassy was electric, as the Ambassador's wife with lots of helpers came to the camp with books, clothes, sweets, food etc. and generally made life much easier to bear for the inmates.

When we had arrived at Medouna we all had a medical inspection, and by this time my nose was going nicely septic (it must have been missing its daily salt douche in sea water, as the water in the camp was apallingly bad). My nose was also very smelly, and the French Medical officer took one sniff and said, 'Hôpital pour vous'. With Wing Commander Mears who had stove in his ribs I was taken in a prison van, complete with guard, to the Casablanca Hospital. There was no need for the guard as we were too weak to run off! I might say the prison cage in which we travelled resembled a huge meat safe on wheels, and was pulled by two mules! The hospital was L'Hôpital Militaire and its Commander, or Médecin-Chef, was Colonel Ribolet. He was quite charming and very efficient, and although he spoke no English and used an interpreter, he was obviously pro-British. He informed me he was going to recommend that I be repatriated through France, along with a Canadian pilot who had been shot down over Casablanca Bay and had lost a leg. Alan Bell was his name: he had been in the hospital for four months and was delighted to have someone to speak to. As he'd been in for some time he was getting some Red Cross parcels through, and he was able to spare me a shirt which was a pleasant change from my silk pyjamas, which after continuous washings were wearing very thin!

From my arrival in the hospital things started to look up. Not only was I cheered by the thought of my repatriation but Alan was great company, with a huge sense of humour, and because of his lengthy stay in the hospital he had acquired quite a bit of French, unlike me, who didn't understand the French nurses' instructions. Luckily I had had to take the temperatures of horses when I was a groom pre-war, and when I tried to take mine orally only to see there was vaseline on the thermometer I knew enough to realise that the French, as usual, get things arsey-tarsy and take one's temperature at the other end! As the hospital was for all military personnel we had in there a member of the German Control Commission, which virtually controlled the whole of Casablanca, and Alan and I had the greatest fun making life as unpleasant for him as we could. He couldn't retaliate because officially they shouldn't have been in Casa!

After the American Ambassador found out about the Brits in the camp he heard about us in the hospital and got a lovely old Sussex lady, well into her seventies, to come to see what we needed. Mrs Paton-Bethune was a gem, and I'm only sad that I was never able to make contact with her post-war. As I was to be repatriated through France in November, with a five day wartime journey to Lisbon, she was determined to get me warm clothes. The suit she produced was of sackcloth, I've bagged tatties in better! She got me two pairs of socks, one thick and one thin. As always my feet were the problem, as they are size twelve, and I finished up with a pair of boots made of some sort of paper material: I hoped I wasn't to encounter too much wet weather in France! My tie, I remember, was yellow with red spots, a present from the Americans to Alan! On 19 October the Médecin-Chef came in with a bottle of brandy. Through his interpreter he told us we were to board a ship next day for Marseilles, he wished us well and we drank each others' health.

We got down to the docks next day only to be told the ship was full of people who were being evacuated from Dakar. It transpired the Germans and Vichy French thought that's where the North African landings were going to take place. With heavy hearts Alan and I were taken back to the hospital, little realising what a lucky escape we had had. Lucky, because had we gone on that ship we would have landed in Southern France just before the North African landings which turned the whole German occupation of France into turmoil. I heard afterwards that immediately after the landings the Germans, who had previously only occupied Northern France, took over the whole of France, and got very tough with people like ourselves trying to be re-patriated via the Red Cross. But as you will read, my luck was to be in yet again. They say it is better to be born lucky than good looking, and at that time I certainly wasn't the latter!

We gradually saw how much control the Germans had over the French in Casablanca. The American Ambassador's wife, who was so good to us, said she just loved driving around in the Embassy's big Buick car, as the head of the German Control Commission also drove around in one. All the German troops, and there were all too many, used to salute her thinking she was in the German car, only to get the 'V' sign in reply. And old Mrs Paton-Bethune just loved the fact that at her age, over seventy, she couldn't be interned, and so cocked a snook at the Germans as only the British could do in this so-called neutral zone. During that stay in hospital, through meeting the Médecin-Chef, the nurses and the other inmates, even with my useless schoolboy French, I realised how the Germans had deviously, through the Vichy French, taken over Casablanca.

When Alan and I got back to the hospital it was clear that all realised invasion was in the air, the only question was where or when? It was a strange thing that the fortnight between the time we were meant to leave and when we actually did so, 20 October to 4 November, we were treated better than ever before. Was it a coincidence or did they think the Allies might win after all? At the same period, according to Molly, the smarmy French Commander of the camp (with his concubines) said, 'You will tell the invading forces how good we've been to you?' Remembering how this guy had stopped their mail home, not allowed them basics like soap, towels, books etc. she replied 'We'll tell them!' But I think what she told them would be different from what he wanted!

These days of waiting were some of the most frustrating I had in the war. They always say war is ninety per cent boredom and ten per cent action but this wait was one hundred per cent boredom. Wing Commander Mears was sadly not fit enough to join us, but wrote a letter to his sister telling her to give me a slap-up dinner at Scott's which sadly I've never managed to take up! Alan, Wing Commander Mears and I had been extremely lucky to be in the hospital compared with those in the camp. As the patients there were mostly French officers, our food was as good as they could provide, but Mrs Paton-Bethune and the Médecin-Chef both told us it was shocking the amount that was being shipped out to Germany via France. When eventually Alan and I got away the ship on which we travelled was full of vegetables and pigs, dozens if not hundreds of them living below decks in conditions that would put modern animal activists off pork and bacon eating for life! My lasting memory of that hospital stay was the anti-British feeling of the French officers. They just didn't want to know us, and did their best to be awkward to Alan and me which upset Colonel Ribolet terribly, as he was sure the Allies would win at the end of the day and was a dedicated follower of De Gaulle and the Free French.

On 5 November we got the glad news that we were about to board a Messagerie Maritime line boat called *L'Eridan*. My papers were marked 'Lille', where I was to go before a Red Cross Medical Board to see if I was to be repatriated via Lisbon, or not. When Alan and I went on board we were sent for by the skipper, who left us in no doubts where his leanings were, with the Nazis. He told us we could have the run of the ship during the day but at night we would be locked in our cabin, and that during the day we would have an interpreter with us. The latter was easy to come by on that ship, as pre-war she had been on the Marseilles to Australia run. The chief steward was half-Australian and openly pro-Allied and fed us grapes and wine, with strict instructions to chuck the pips and empty bottles out of the porthole during the night. Alan and I hadn't been fed so well for months, and couldn't believe our luck. *L'Eridan* was part of a small convoy of coastal vessels and hugged the North African coastline. It went very slowly, but our pal the steward assured us that once we got to Oran we would ditch the rest of the convoy and go full steam ahead for Marseilles. There was a charming French Professor from the Sorbonne on board. He and his wife had been having a short holiday in Morocco, and he was dreading going back to France. He just hated the Germans, and although he had a house in the south of France which up until the North African landing was meant to be outwith German control, the Professor said it was, like Morocco, being milked of all its farm produce, and if local mayors didn't cooperate they just disappeared! He was most disappointed that we didn't know when the invasion of Europe would take place. As far as he was concerned he wanted to see 'the laughing Tommies and the piping Jocks' back again, and these were his own words as he had excellent English. I by this time was writing down the odd snippet for an article, little dreaming it would be needed for a book fifty-three years on! Though it very nearly wouldn't have been needed if the skipper had had his way.

Our steward told us when we were about to pass Gibraltar, and we watched a British destroyer take a turn out to inspect our wee convoy from afar. We hoped and prayed he'd come over and sort us all out, but of course France was meant to be our ally. What a devious lot the Vichy French were, and after all these fifty-plus years I find it hard to forgive them. At least with the Germans, even those dedicated U-boat commanders said, 'We don't agree with all Hitler's plans, but we're Germans, and we fight for our homeland and must remain united'. But the Vichy French were willing to ally themselves with whichever side they thought would do them most good. I found them a despicable lot and rotten to the core, but strangely enough I never came across what I call a 'Jock', a ranker, who was a committed Vichy supporter: it was always the 'officer class'.

On the third night on board, about 3 a.m., the whole ship shivered and

Alan was thrown out of his bunk. I thought, and said to him, 'Torpedoed again, and here we are caught like rats in a trap thanks to that bastard of a Vichy skipper'. But our super steward knew about our predicament, and was down to unlock our cabin door within minutes as he knew his skipper had far too much on his plate to worry about his prisoners. Moving Alan with his wooden leg in a hurry was not easy, but after much puffing and shoving and blowing I got him 'topsides' as the Navy say, i.e. on deck. There we saw one of the finest sights it's ever been my pleasure to witness, a British Hunt Class destroyer which had rammed us. How was our Vichy skipper to know he was to get in the way of the North African landing? And who was he to think he could 'cock a snook' at the British Navy and get away with it, which is what he tried to do? Unbeknown to him he had landed smack in the middle of the North African landing. When he had been ordered to stop his small convoy, he had refused and so was rammed by a destroyer. Standing on deck I said to Alan, 'Not twice, thank God', and I meant it, as my maker has given me another marvellous fifty-plus years since that night, when for the fourth time the Axis forces tried to get shot of me.

It was just marvellous next morning when we were allowed out to see the sight that met our 'sore eyes'. Destroyers, mine sweepers and a big ship, the *Princess Beatrix*, which we found out later had the landing craft on board in which the Americans were to storm the North African beaches! They wouldn't realise until years later that this was to be the easiest landing they were to be asked to do compared with the Pacific island landings.

I was sent for by Commander Brunton of the *Princess Beatrix*, who was senior officer in the bay. Also with me were the Captain of *L'Eridan* and his first officer, covered, I might say, with a revolver held by a young R.N.V.R. lieutenant who it turned out was a friend of my youngest brother. It's the old story, it's not what you know it's who you know, and he smoothed my passage for the next week!

It turned out the skipper was really nasty and tried to cut up rough with Commander Brunton, who stood no nonsense and just sent him under guard to one of the oil tankers who were backing up the landing team, and that's the last that was heard of him! Meantime the Commander said that I should go back to *L'Eridan*, with its first officer, and bring back Alan. He, the Commander, would see that Alan with his peg leg would be properly handled. When we got back to *L'Eridan* I couldn't believe my ears when the First Lieutenant ordered me to go below to my cabin and be locked in with Alan, as he meant to make a run for it. To say it was a foolhardy decision is putting it mildly, with the number of British destroyers swanning around, but luckily the First Lieutenant didn't know that the Captain, before he was ordered off the ship, had told the Chief Engineer to sabotage the engines!

The next morning Commander Brunton sent over a boarding party. Those of us of my vintage will remember at the beginning of the war there was a ship called the *Altmark* in Norway, which was being used as a P.O.W. camp, and a British force boarded it, led I think by Commander Vian V.C., and went below shouting 'Any British here?' Well, the same thing happened to us, as the search and rescue party kept shouting 'Where are you?' until they found us where we were locked up. The Lieutenant R.N. in charge of the party, like all of us of that age group, had seen Western films where the hero shoots the lock off a door and was longing to use his service revolver for the first time. He was not amused when the bullet ricocheted! But luckily our pro-Allied steward came to the rescue with the key. The Commander then put a squad of Americans on board to keep law and order.

Alan and I were taken off, which took a bit of time. As I had told them on the *Princess Beatrix* that there was a Canadian pilot with one leg along with me, the Commander had ordered his Medical Officer, Dr Jack Armstrong (whose memory of this period is better than mine) to take two Sick Bay Attendants plus a Neil Robertson stretcher with them as Alan with his peg leg couldn't negotiate ship's ladders etc. Jack Armstrong, who I am glad to say is still fit and well in Yorkshire, is one of the few I have kept in touch with since the end of the war. He says he had never used one of those stretchers before and he and his S.B.A.s were terrified when they swung it overboard that Alan would slip out as do the coffins when there is a burial at sea.

However all was well and Alan and I had those wonderful days watching the start of an invasion of a country held by the enemy. The Americans at that landing had all the ground troops and the British were supplying the naval forces, the landing craft and associated personnel. Commander Brunton interviewed Alan and me and was so kind to us: however he said, 'You can stay with us as long as we're not in the action, but if we are I must move you on'. He also, very rightly, said he wanted us vetted by Jack Armstrong, his Medical Officer. Jack probably doesn't remember, but he found that I had picked up scabies, either on *La Gloire* or more likely in Medouna Camp. The cure is to use a strong scrubbing brush to get rid of the scabs, and then to put on something that hurts like hell. Alan of course, apart from his 'Long John Silver' leg was fit as a flea. The whole crew of *Princess Beatrix* were

A scene from the African Landings. One of the British landing barges, the white LCMB, similar to the one we helped to salvage, is seen in the centre. One can see there was no resistance on this beach

quite marvellous to us, as up to then they hadn't been actually in the war, although they had been training hard for months for this landing, learning lessons from the disastrous Dieppe effort where the combatants had got a very different reception.

When we got on board Alan realised why he had been shot down, as he had been photographing all the beaches that were to be used, or not used, in the North African landings. What bliss it was to be with people who spoke the same language, ate the same sort of food, enjoyed a 'wee dram', or in their case, being Navy, gin! It was then that my old cavalry greatcoat really came into its own, thanks to George Munn's instructions about having a haversack packed in case of torpedoing or any other emergency. He told us always to have some money available and to patch it into our clothing if necessary. Accordingly I had stitched into the lining of my greatcoat one of those lovely old white English fivers, which was big money in those days. With gin or any other drink at that time, including Drambuie, selling at five old pennies (two and a half pence today!) each, we were able to stand the Officers' Mess drinks all round as they had been our liberators.

What a wonderful scene that was to see those landing craft to-ing and fro-ing from the *Princess Beatrix* laden with heavily armed American troops. One felt elation at being present at the opening scene of America's participation in the war, and my goodness at that stage especially how much we needed them and their wonderful equipment. So for a few days Alan and I enjoyed a view from the 'stalls' of the North African landings.

Twelve
'TORCH' (THE NORTH AFRICAN LANDING), ORAN AND HOSPITAL

Those days on the *Princess Beatrix* were to remain in my memory as some of the most outstanding I had in the war. Several things contributed to this—the change from being a prisoner of war, being back with one's ain folk, having good food, good drink, good companionship and most of all, knowing that the Yanks were not just 'coming' but were here, at least supporting us if not yet fighting, so that it looked at last no matter how long it took we could win.

The *Princess Beatrix* was a converted Dutch cross-channel ferry which had come out with Naval personnel on board plus their landing craft, and five hundred and fifty U.S. troops whom they were to disembark on the North African coast. It seems there had been fifty to sixty ships in the original convoy, but after passing Gibraltar they had split into smaller groups of five or six ships, and the *Princess Beatrix*, with a Polish liner *Batory*, a converted oil tanker carrying tanks, plus a couple of corvettes and a Hunt Class destroyer, headed for a bay west of Oran. They had been due to arrive there at midnight when they came across our French convoy crawling along the coast. It seems two of the French convoy were so scared they beached themselves, and as I've already written the skipper of *L'Eridan* was as bolshie as he could be.

Actually in this bay there was no opposition to the landings to speak of, and just as well, as the Yanks at that time had never seen any action and were green as the proverbial grass. They gave cigarettes out all round, then stacked their rifles against buildings and wondered why they weren't there when they came back! You name it, they contravened everything we in the British Army had been trained to do. But honour where honour is due, look how General Patton's forces fought up from the south of France, and who in their right senses would have liked to do that ghastly island hopping in the Pacific under General Douglas McArthur? But at that time, to use their own expression, 'they sure were green'.

All the naval side was British-controlled and officered, but they too weren't all seasoned sailors, and not being helped by some very nasty weather they had quite a job getting all the tanks and equipment ashore. Some of the L.C.T.s were overturned in the storm, and a team was sent from the *Princess Beatrix* to see if they could be righted. I wangled my way into the team (which I had no right to do) as I wanted a swim! And how super it was.

As has happened to me so many times in my life I had met someone who knew either my family or someone who knew someone. Scotland is not a large country, and pre-war the people looked up to were the doctors, the dominies (the teaching profession) and the clergy, of which Father was a well known member. He made his name as a first-class preacher, never giving more than a ten minute sermon, over which he sweated blood, but he was probably best known as one who didn't want to be the Moderator of the Church of Scotland because he thought the headquarters at 121 George Street held too much sway. Nothing alters! Through the Church connection, as I mentioned in the last chapter, I was recognised by one of the young Naval lieutenants who was not only a Scot but had been at some Scottish Church camp with my youngest brother where Dad had been involved. He it was who took me on that super trip to try to right the L.C.T. Jack Armstrong swears that I wanted to dive under it; I was a strong though slow swimmer, but this I can't believe as the one experience I had of my half nose being immersed was not something I'd like to repeat. Another officer I got on terribly well with was a Canadian, one Al Gardiner. This meeting had an amazing sequel. Al was a timber expert and after the war married a lovely English Rose and they decided to go to Australia where Al did extremely well in the timber business. I had kept his address and was in Sydney on a Nuffield Agricultural Scholarship in 1964, and having a day to spare phoned him up. As is my wont I said I wanted to go to church and then could I visit him? He gave me the instructions, which train to get, where the church was, and how to get to him. When I arrived, and we hadn't seen each other for twenty-odd years, he had an apron on his broad frame and was cooking a barbecue, and in his right hand he held a glass that to me seemed to contain a large pink gin. After the introductions to his family and neighbours were completed he said, 'What are you going to drink, Ben?' and I said 'The same as you, Al'. To which he replied, 'But you've just been to the Australian Presbyterian Church [please forgive me any members if I've got the name wrong] they are all teetotallers and I'm drinking pink gin'. (Angostura Bitters, gin and water to those who are not fortunate enough to have enjoyed this excellent pre-prandial drink.) 'I could see that', said I. From that day to the day he died Al and I kept contact. This continued to the next generation. Shaun, my second son, whom I had organised to go to Australia in the last of the cattle boats via New Zealand, mucked up his back riding in a calf-cutting competition, an event like an American rodeo. Anyway, his back was so bad he was sent to this super hospital near Sydney, and it was so close to Al's abode you would think it was organised on purpose! Shaun had been sent hundreds of miles to this hospital and was visited regularly there by Al and his family, in fact I suspect that Shaun and one of Al's daughters were rather fond of each other.

Al is no longer with us, but before he died I introduced him to my old boss's whisky 'McCallum's Perfection', which is a great seller in Australia, and I only hope it didn't hasten his demise. Of the staff of the *Princess Beatrix*, whom I understand had reunions for many years, Dr Armstrong is still going strong. But what a marvellous bunch they were. This was brought home to me, as an outsider looking in, as one who had seen his regiment fighting for every inch at Keren, taken part in one of the worst sinkings of the war, and witnessed how at that time the Brits could, as former civilians, come up trumps. This was highlighted for me by what I saw of that so-called North African landing on our beach where the American troops, who like us were mostly pre-war civilians, had no discipline whatsoever, and had there been any opposition they would have had a fearful drubbing.

But back to my story. All good things come to an end, and after some idyllic days on the *Princess Beatrix* spent bathing, using up some of my lovely English fiver (Drambuie at 5d. a glass!) Commander Brunton received orders to proceed to Oran and then Algiers. First he had to take two hundred U.S. troops from the Polish liner *Batory*. No sooner had that order been obeyed, and transferring that number is not easy, than a counter order came through, 'Transfer them to HMS *Sheffield*'. There's an old Army saying, 'one order plus one counter order equals disorder'! How true.

So off we sailed for Oran, where I saw one of the finest sights to greet my eyes since that magical sight of Cape Town all lit up two years previously. It was a harbour jam-packed with Allied shipping. There was a cruiser or two, destroyers, mine-sweepers and in the harbour itself converted liners that had brought the Americans to North Africa. When the *Princess Beatrix* berthed Commander Brunton sent for me and said, 'I'm very sorry, Ben, but we have orders to sail for Bone further east, and as it's in 'bomb alley' [i.e.

within reach of Axis bombers] you and Alan as non-combatants would be an embarrassment to us. But there are lots of Army personnel in the town. Off you go and organise a trip home'.

So I set off up the town, and must have looked very conspicuous in my sackcloth suit, my spotted tie, a large swab where my nose should have been and those 'herring boxes without topsies' that were my footwear. Anyway in a very short time a typical 'Jock', Glengarry all askew, smoking a cigarette and driving a five hundred-weight truck drew up and asked where I was going. On being briefly told my story he said, 'Jump in and I'll take you to Army Headquarters', which were of course in what had been the best hotel in the town. When he dumped me there I had a job getting past the guard because of my bizarre clothing, but because of my voice, and how often in my life I have had to thank it, he let me past to see the officer in charge of administration, who was a Guards Officer. When I stood in front of him and explained that I wanted to get home he brusquely said, 'We're disembarking troops here not embarking them, you realise there's a war on'. I'm usually a placid sort of a chap but I suddenly saw red, pulled off my nose dressing revealing a rather messy gap where there should have been a bridge and said, 'Yes, I collected this lot in Tobruk Garrison while you were swanning about in Bird Cage Walk'. The poor chap went white at the gills, but I left smartly. I didn't want to be interned because I had no papers to prove my identity.

Getting out into the street I cooled down and was considering what to do, when my super friend the 'Jock', with yet another fag hanging from the corner of his mouth, came up again in his five hundred-weight truck. God knows what he was meant to be doing, but as far as I was concerned he was heaven-sent. I told him what had happened and we decided we should go back to the harbour, not the one where the *Princess Beatrix* had berthed, with the combatant vessels, but the big one where all the liners lay, to see if one wouldn't take Alan and me home. The first vessel I set my eyes on was the *Stratheden*, which as you have read I had been on from Suez to Durban. I may have had some bad luck but I've also had more than my share of good luck, and finding the *Stratheden* in Oran was quite extraordinary to say the least. What a welcome I got from the skipper and crew, as they were sure I would have been one of the two thousand that were lost on the *Laconia* because of my half nose. They had heard about the *Laconia* sinking because Grizel, being the Earl of Glasgow's daughter, was reported missing suspected drowned after Freckles' lifeboat made land. To add to my luck the liaison Army officer on board the *Stratheden* who was responsible for cash was a Glasgow Academical and remembered me, and so I got some much needed 'lolly'. Yet again it was the old story 'it's who you know'.

So it was back to the *Princess Beatrix* to collect Alan and to thank Commander Brunton and his super team for their kindness to us. That ship and the way it was run, mostly by amateur sailors, demonstrated to me what, if one has a good leader and a keen hard-working team, can be accomplished. This is as true today as it was in wartime, but sadly the leaders are getting few and far between as greed has taken a hold. When I got back to the *Princess Beatrix* for Alan it turned out I was just in time as she had her sailing orders for Bone. Again Jack Armstrong and his S.B.A.s moved Alan, this time with jokes all round as they had got to know each other.

With money in our pockets and two days in Oran harbour, at the time of year that people nowadays choose to go there because in November the climate is ideal, Alan and I lived the life of Riley! I have no doubts our stories, after a drink or two, got more and more distant from the truth. Alan's were about his ignorance of the job he was doing, which of course was to photograph the landing beaches, his long stay in L'Hôpital Militaire, his amputation and subsequent wooden leg, but best of all his admiration for the American Ambassador's wife who brought him all the 'goodies' she could spare. She was a wonderful lady, who as I have described used to cock a snook at the Germans. She didn't care a damn for them and used to tell them so, and on occasions had to be reprimanded by her husband for going too far. I'm only sorry I wasn't in Casablanca when the Yanks took over the town, I'll bet she had a ball. She would have got her own back on all the Jerries, and they were the nasty ones, being 'desk wallahs', not fighting types like the U-boat commanders. And as for me, I suppose I banged on about the torpedoing etc. The *Stratheden* crew for their part had been lucky, and well-manned, and hadn't had a crisis.

The sad thing for me looking back, and a half century is a long time in anyone's lifespan, is that of those lovely people who were so good to me only Jack Armstrong is left with whom I have contact. How I would have liked to meet Alan Bell again, or the American Ambassador's wife or Mrs Paton-Bethune, though as she was over seventy when I was in Casa that was impossible. After the war we were all so busy making new lives for ourselves, getting jobs, re-adjusting to civvy street, marrying, procreating, you name it, we were so busy we lost touch with our wartime pals.

After two days the *Stratheden*'s skipper got the order to join a convoy outside Algiers and we were on our way home. For the whole journey Alan and I wore our lifebelts—it didn't make sleep any easier but we knew if we

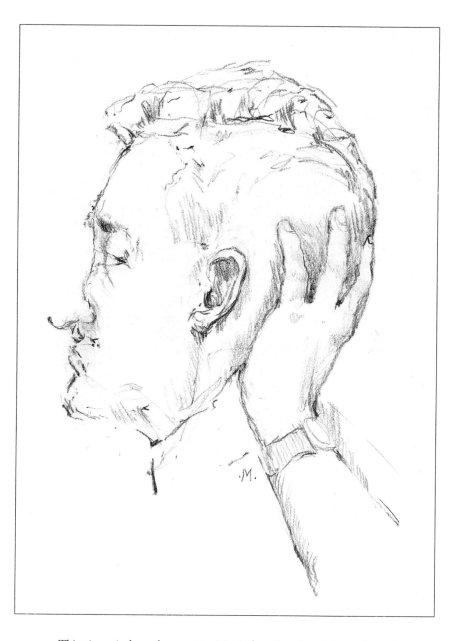

This picture is drawn by my sister Maisie from the original photo taken of me when I was admitted with my facial wound to No.8 General Hospital Alexandria. I had detached the photo from my medical files to show to someone on board the Laconia, and as a result it was in my greatcoat pocket and got soaked in too much 'saline solution' to be reproduced here

got a 'tin fish' into the *Stratheden* at least we would be prepared. I couldn't get over the cover we had, Allied aircraft flying overhead, which we could dearly have done with in East Africa and the desert, but at that time we just didn't have the planes or the pilots. Then we had a cruiser, some destroyers, corvettes—oh, just everything one who had been torpedoed would want to see guarding a convoy. I only wish we had video cameras in those days, not that I'm any good with these modern gadgets, but it was a magnificent sight, and the Mediterranean light at that time of year is something special. Entirely different to the light we were to see when, ten days later, we anchored in the Clyde. The Argyll hills had their first coating of snow and the air was as clear as crystal.

As written up in *Bothy to Big Ben* I was extremely lucky to get to East Grinstead under Archie McIndoe. Nowadays people say to me seeing the large scar on my forehead, 'Did you have a motor accident?' or 'Did you box in your younger days, as your nose looks like that of a pugilist?' But what they see is the result of brilliant plastic surgery.

I had to undergo an operation called a 'Rhinoplasty', which means that the surgeon, having had one's hair completely removed, then cuts the area from the forehead required to cover the part of the nose that is missing. To keep the blood and nerves flowing without interruption, this area of tissue must be kept in contact with the person's body, so the surgeon has to cut a sausage-like portion off the top of one's head, where there is not much flesh, then turn it round, rather like an elephant's trunk, and affix it to the bottom of one's nose. After, I think, a couple of weeks, the nerves, arteries, veins etc. have taken in the transplanted skin, so the surgeon then cuts off the amount of replacement nose he wants and flips the rest back onto one's head, where after fifty years I grow more hair than my younger brother! Quite honestly I think I have kept my hair because of the number of times my head was shaved. Once the gap at the top of my nose was covered, so to speak, bone had to be replaced to hold up the 'new' nose. To this day I wonder at the amazing accuracy that Archie had on (a) how much skin he needed from one's forehead to cover the gap and (b) how much extra he needed to allow him to insert the amount of bone required. The bone was literally chiselled from my hips, and was mashed up, which the great man told me made a firmer job than just putting in a whole piece of bone. What amazed me about this operation, quite the most painful I endured, was that he cut my 'new' nose straight down the middle, but I'd defy anyone to see a stitch-mark. His stitches were fantastic: I don't know how many hundred he told me I'd had on my old face, but I can't see a sign of one and I see my

The author on his farm in Upper Speyside after his final trimming operation by the one and only Archie McIndoe. Sir Archie completed his reconstruction of the author's nose the year before he died

face each morning when I shave.

I can't say how lucky I am that my wound has given me so little trouble after all these years, apart from the odd blockage. I can no longer blow my nose as any ordinary person can do, so that every now and then I have to give myself one of those famous saline douches recommended all those years ago to remove the gubbage. I have no feeling in much of my nose and also in my top lip, and as in the last fifty years my nose can suddenly bleed I always carry a red handkerchief. When I'm asked why, as a Liberal, I sport Labour colours, I always answer 'It's handy for a bleeding nose and removing lipstick stains'—but sadly at my age it is no longer needed for the latter! One thing I can be thankful for after all the operations is that when I was wounded the shrapnel removed bits of my teeth and left nasty roots, all of which eventually had to be removed and replaced by 'snappers'. My mother was terribly upset about this as she said I had the most lovely set of teeth. Little did she know how much pain those 'lovely' teeth had given me, as, being reared in the Glasgow area where the water is infamous for being bad for teeth, mine were as soft as putty and I was never out of the dentist's chair and had constant toothache. So Hitler, you did me one favour, even if getting the roots removed was painful.

Of course all the operations were painful, and the only reason I mention them is that those hospital years were all part of my wartime experiences. I realise every day when I walk out of my back door first thing in the morning and look to the hills 'from whence doth come mine aid' how lucky I have been. Thousands had worse war experiences than I had. Thousands paid the supreme sacrifice. But in this year of the fiftieth anniversary of the Victory in Europe some people thought that my wartime experiences might be of interest. There can't be a lot of us who cheated death four times. A member of the Royal Family, on being told that I was present at a certain prestigious gathering, said, 'What, that old rogue?' Rogue I know I may be, but having come through what I have tried to describe above and having had a Christian upbringing from Father, I try to be in my church pew each Sunday to thank God for allowing me still to be 'in the breathing business'.